The Challenge of Teaching Social Studies
in the Elementary School

The Challenge

DOROTHY J. SKEEL, *Indiana University*

Goodyear Publishing Company, Inc.
Pacific Palisades, California

# of Teaching Social Studies
in the Elementary School

**THE CHALLENGE OF TEACHING SOCIAL STUDIES
IN THE ELEMENTARY SCHOOL**

Dorothy J. Skeel

© 1970 by
GOODYEAR PUBLISHING COMPANY, INC.
Pacific Palisades, California

LIBRARY OF CONGRESS CATALOG CARD NUMBER: 77-83543

Current printing (last number): 10 9 8 7 6 5

PRINTED IN THE UNITED STATES OF AMERICA

Preface

TEACHING SOCIAL STUDIES IN THE ELEMENTARY SCHOOL PRE-
sents a challenge to any teacher, new or experienced. This
challenge results from the unique content of the social
studies and its contribution to our democratic way of living.
The content of the social studies is derived from the social
sciences, which investigate the actions of human beings. In
teaching social studies, teachers attempt to help children
understand the actions of human beings (from the earliest
times to the present) to prepare the children to enter their
society with sufficient knowledge to enable them to operate
effectively within it. Our democratic form of government
requires that its citizens be knowledgeable about democracy
as well as the other ideologies. The responsibility of impart-
ing this knowledge rests heavily with the social studies.

These challenges would be sufficient without the added
concern of selecting appropriate content, teaching methods,
and materials to successfully achieve the goals of social

studies in the elementary school. The wide divergency of current social studies curricula, the many suggested methods of teaching, and an abundance of available materials confounds the teacher's task. This text is designed to aid teachers in teaching social studies by presenting the current thinking on content, teaching methods, and available materials.

The text first discusses the importance of social studies in preparing children to enter the mainstream of society. Second, the text delineates social studies programs that have been prepared at the local, state, and national level, discussing their rationale, content, method, and materials. Next, several methods of teaching social studies—including problem solving through inquiry, unit development, method from the structure of the social science disciplines, and method for teaching the disadvantaged—are discussed.

The second half of the text presents activities for practical application of the theories in teaching current affairs, international understandings, skill development in committee work, and map and globe skills. Also included is a discussion of the selection and utilization of materials and of the important aspect of evaluation of social studies instruction at the classroom, local, state, and national level.

I want to acknowledge the assistance of the following in the preparation of my manuscript: James P. Levy, Diana P. O'Connor, Sharon Fox, Dr. Barbara Frey, Dr. V. Phillips Weaver, and Louise Hansen.

Dorothy J. Skeel

Contents

To Jeff, Shelly, and Jill—

May their world of tomorrow be an exciting,
stimulating place to live.

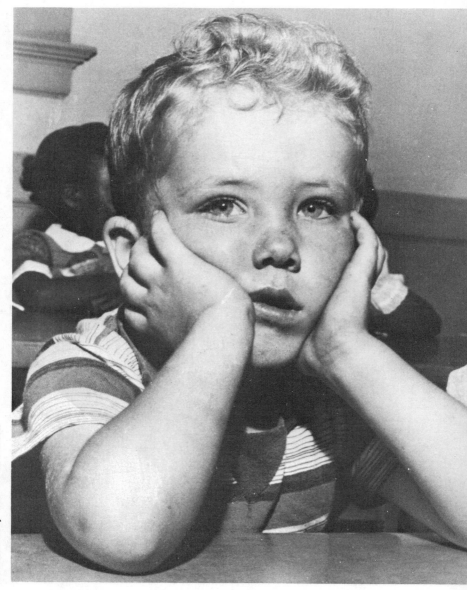

What does the world of tomorrow offer him?

Introduction

WHAT IS SOCIAL STUDIES? WHAT PURPOSE DOES THIS SUBJECT serve in the elementary-school curriculum? Teachers repeatedly ask these questions as they contemplate planning a program of learning experiences for children. The complicated problem of combining the proper mixture of reading, writing, arithmetic, science, art, music, health, physical education, and numerous other suggested activities leaves many teachers bewildered. They wonder how social studies can be included in an already crowded schedule and, even more relevant, if the subject is really that important.

Part one attempts to answer these questions by discussing the meaning of social studies and its role in preparing children for the world of tomorrow. The development of objectives in the social studies is discussed in behavioral or performance terms. This section also outlines social studies programs that have been established at local, state, and national levels and delineates the rationale, objectives, sample content, and activities of each program.

CHAPTER ONE

What Is Social Studies?

WHERE ARE THE LEADERS OF THE TWENTY-FIRST CENTURY? Where are the presidents, the world statesmen, the Supreme Court Justices, the doctors, the scientists, the teachers, the clergy, the union bosses? Where are the other citizens of the twenty-first century? Are they beginning school this year? How will our schools prepare these leaders and citizens for the roles they will eventually assume?

Can educators comprehend what the world of that century will be like? Will there be interplanetary travel and habitation? What forms of government will be in existence? Will men of all races and creeds truly live together as brothers? What will remain of our natural resources? Will man's labor consist of pushing buttons in a mechanistic age? Will disease be conquered? Will man's life span be increased? What forms of aesthetic expression will be prevalent?

Although answers to these questions are not known today,

the questions complicate the problems facing our schools. With the rapid technological and social changes occurring today, the status of the world of tomorrow is relatively unknown. How can our schools prepare children for the future? Will reading, writing, and mathematics be sufficient? What does the area of social studies offer?

What is social studies? Social studies is an investigation of human actions, in the rain-swept tropics of Africa, in the frozen tundra of the Arctic, in the hustle and bustle of the many large cities of the world, as well as in the small towns and rural areas. It is the study of man busily engaged in the processes of life: providing food, clothing, and shelter for himself and others by using the available resources; communicating and getting along with his fellow men; propagating his race; using and attempting to improve upon the tools and heritage of his past; organizing and protecting his institutions; expressing himself aesthetically; enjoying himself; solving the problems of his labor and everyday living; and educating those who will soon take over his tasks.

If social studies is defined as the study of human actions and deemed essential in preparing the individual for the next century, how can this knowledge be imparted to the young? How can they learn to appreciate the hardship, labor, love, and battle required of generations past in providing our heritage? How can they comprehend the magnitude of the interrelationships existing among the nations of the world? How can they understand the delicate balance of patience, understanding, and tact essential to the development of good human relationships? How can they learn to appreciate the aesthetic qualities of the elements in their environment? Should teachers present a hierarchy of the concepts of the social sciences? Should they teach children to solve problems? Should teachers shower students with as much available knowledge as possible? Should they teach children about cultures other than their own?

No one can argue the value of social studies in the elementary curriculum in helping prepare citizens of the twenty-first century. Consider, for example, the momentous problems that must be faced by both present and future citizens of the United States: the problems of racial strife that tear apart its urban areas; the pockets of poverty that deprive many of its people of an acceptable existence; and the tremendous responsibility of using its resources to provide military and economic aid to the developing countries of the world. Such a nation requires its schools to prepare youth who can understand and cope with these and similar problems. The continued existence of the United States as a free democratic nation depends upon the ability of future generations to perpetuate and protect its ideals. The social studies area is the source from which the necessary understandings, attitudes, and abilities for such perpetuation can be fostered.

Because social studies is such an essential subject, the method of communicating it must be carefully considered. What is the best method of teaching social studies in the elementary school? Is one method more effective than another, or should a combination of methods be used? This text does not intend to promote one method over another. Instead, it presents the philosophy and procedure of several current methods and suggests that teachers select the method that proves most effective for them and their students.

Objectives of the Social Studies

The objectives specified for a social studies curriculum will vary in accordance with the educator's viewpoint concerning the major purpose of social studies. An educator may consider this major purpose to be the development of skill in understanding human relationships, the acquiring of the skills of the social scientists, the development of skill in solving problems, or a combination of these. Whatever purpose the teacher selects, his choice will determine the objectives of his program. If he sees the main purpose of the social studies as a responsibility to help children develop skill in and an understanding of human relationships, his broad objectives would necessarily be:

To develop the student's ability to work cooperatively in a group toward the completion of a task.

To increase the student's understanding of the varying abilities of individuals and of the worth of each individual.

To encourage the student's understanding of his own culture and of the cultures of the world and to develop his appreciation for the contributions of each culture to our heritage.

To develop the student's skill in the art of communicating with others through verbal and nonverbal means.

However, if the educator views the purpose of social study as Clements, Fielder, and Tabachnick to be,

The process of learning about variety and change in the actions of people as they arrange to live together in groups. This learning goes on through the gathering of social data, as well as through critical examination of the conclusions and generalizations of social scientists.[1]

[1]H. Millard Clements, William R. Fielder, and B. Robert Tabachnick, *Social Study: Inquiry in Elementary Classrooms* (Indianapolis: The Bobbs-Merrill Company, Inc., 1966), p. 13.

his goals might be:

To develop in children the ability to evaluate interpretation, i.e., to use evidence to test ideas.

To provide children with the opportunity to write about how they think and feel about the world in which they live.

To lead individuals to examine the circumstances of their lives, to question the values they have been taught, to become to some extent responsible for their own views.

To develop the ability to use primary documents, a variety of interpretations of past and present events, records, and artifacts that relate what has been and is going on in the world.[2]

If the main purpose of social studies is thought to be the presentation of the concepts of a social science such as the anthropology project of the Education Development Center, the objectives are stated thus:

To confront children with a number of opportunities to observe and ponder about the lives of other animals to help them think concretely about what it means to be human.

To furnish children with a vocabulary and a frame of reference for thinking about human behavior.

To explore the intriguing fact that survival is a common concern for all living organisms, including man, and that the mechanisms for insuring survival and continuity of life are extremely numerous and diverse.

To reflect upon the extent to which man, in all his cultural diversity, is united by universally adaptive propensities.[3]

The divergence of opinion concerning the purpose of social studies magnifies the task of the teacher. Before he can complete his basic task of determining the objectives of his program and his method of approach, he must first decide what he considers to be the purpose or purposes of social studies. His decision should be based on: (1) the experiential background of the students, (2) the intellectual abilities of the students, (3) the availability of materials necessary for his approach, and (4) the goals for the total curriculum of the school.

[2]H. Millard Clements, "Inquiry and Social Studies," *Elementary English*, March, 1966, pp. 300–301.

[3]Peter B. Dow, "Man: A Course of Study Reexamined," *Teacher Guide, Trial Teaching Edition, Man: A Course of Study* (Cambridge, Mass.: Education Development Center, Inc., 1967). Reprinted by permission of Education Development Center, Inc.

Developing Objectives

Too frequently in the past, objectives have been stated in vague, meaningless, and unmeasurable terms. Currently, however, an increasing number of educators view objectives in terms of behavior or performance, which lend themselves to observation and measurement. Robert Mager defines an objective as,

... an intent communicated by a statement describing a proposed change in a learner—a statement of what the learner is to be like when he has successfully completed a learning experience. It is a description of a pattern of behavior (performance) we want the learner to be able to demonstrate.[4]

Mager indicates the advisability of including the following information when attempting to write objectives in behavioral or performance terms:

First, identify the terminal behavior by name; we can specify the kind of behavior which will be accepted as evidence that the learner has achieved the objective.

Second, try to further define the desired behavior by describing the important conditions under which the behavior will be expected to occur.

Third, specify the criteria of acceptable performance by describing how well the learner must perform to be considered acceptable.[5]

Each objective need not include all of the above information. Initially, objectives are written in broad terms to indicate the type of subject matter to be covered. Secondly, specific objectives are written in behavioral or performance terms to indicate the behavior expected of the individual after he has been exposed to the subject matter. An example of a broad objective is:

To acquire knowledge of the history of Mexico to enable the individual to understand its customs and traditions.

This objective made more specific and stated in behavioral terms might be:

---

[4]Robert F. Mager, *Preparing Instructional Objectives* (Palo Alto, Calif.: Fearon Publishers, Inc., 1962), p. 3.

[5]Mager, *Preparing Instructional Objectives*, p. 12.

To compare and contrast several of the Christmas customs and traditions of Mexico with those of the United States.

To identify two of the traditions sacred to Mexican families.

To list at least one of the Mexican holidays that is different from those celebrated in the United States.

Objectives of the social studies are grouped in four areas: knowledge, understanding, attitudes, and skills. Knowledge and understanding are a part of the cognitive (knowing) domain, attitudes are a part of the affective (emotions or feeling) domain, and skills are an ability or proficiency.

KNOWLEDGE

In the social studies, as in any subject, children should not be required to learn facts or knowledge merely to become walking versions of a book. The knowledge they acquire should be selected on the basis of its capacity to further their understanding. For example, it would be better to learn that Washington became President of the new nation because the people trusted the leadership he exhibited during the Revolution than to merely memorize the fact that he was our first President. Rather than learn the names of the states and their capitals to reel them off in rote fashion it would be better for students to learn that state capitals are generally located near the center of the states to better serve the people of that state.

Objectives developed in the area of knowledge are selected to further an understanding. An example of such an objective would be:

To gain knowledge of the minority groups of the United States to better understand how much they contribute to our society.

UNDERSTANDING

One of the most important aspects of the social studies is the area of understanding. Obviously, facts are of little value unless they increase one's understanding of a subject or problem. Understanding requires the individual to synthesize several pieces of information, relating them to one another to comprehend the connection between his previous knowledge and the newly acquired information. Understanding of a problem is essential before an individual can attempt to solve it. With understanding, various pieces of information can be fitted together for a possible solution.

Measurement of an individual's achievement in the area of understanding becomes difficult unless the individual applies his new knowledge to a new situation. Therefore, objectives under the heading of understanding must include this application.

Examples of objectives for the area of understanding are:

The student understands that individual abilities differ and shows this understanding by his ready acceptance of people.

He understands that the mobility of people is dependent upon a variety of individual goals such as adventure and greater opportunity, and he recognizes these different goals in a new situation.

ATTITUDES

Attitudes are not actually taught, but they are a by-product of the teaching-learning situation. Attitudes displayed by the behavior of the teacher and peer group affect the attitude of the individual. An attitude is a feeling or emotion, which may be displayed consciously or subconsciously, toward a person, object, or idea. The atmosphere of the classroom affects the attitudes developed. If a teacher is attempting to develop an attitude regarding the importance of the worth of the individual but does not allow each person to express his opinion or does not accept the contributions of each member of the group, it is doubtful that he will convey or instill this attitude in his pupils. Or if a teacher desires to develop a favorable attitude toward a culture other than our own but displays or permits members of the peer group to display obvious dislike of the culture, the achievement of a favorable attitude is unlikely.

Measurement of attitude is best accomplished by observing the behavior of individuals in a given situation. Undoubtedly, there will be occasions when children will display the actions they feel are expected of them, thereby making the measurement of attitude difficult. And there will also be times when teachers misunderstand or misjudge the behavior of children and are unable to assess their real feeling or emotion.

Examples of objectives for the area of attitudes are:

The student appreciates that cooperative behavior is necessary to accomplish certain tasks, and he willingly offers to work with others.

The student values the contributions to our heritage of the many subcultures, and expresses an appreciation for them.

SKILLS

A skill is defined as the ability to become capable or proficient at performing a task or tasks. In stating objectives for this area, the expected capability of the individual should be decided. Because skills are developmental, an acceptable achievement level varies according to the individual's maturation level. For example, a primary-grade child cannot be expected to perform certain skills with the same proficiency as an intermediate-grade child.

Skills are developed sequentially—some must be acquired before others. A child, for example, must learn to read before he can acquire skill in locating information, or he must understand spatial relationships before he can develop skill in map reading. Skills are divided into three subgroups: social, intellectual, and motor.

Social skills are concerned with the interaction of members within a group. Obviously, children who are unable to get along with members of their own class or who constantly display uncooperative behavior will find it difficult to understand and appreciate the necessity for establishing cooperation among other groups or nations. A teacher must first strive to achieve the social skills within the classroom. Objective:

Develop the child's leadership ability by having him assume the role of committee chairman.

Help the child acquire skill in cooperative planning by having him work in committees.

Intellectual skills include skill in research, critical thinking, problem solving, making oral and written reports, outlining, and taking notes. The development of these skills need not be limited to the social studies; they offer an excellent opportunity for integration, especially with the language arts. For example, critical thinking can be introduced in reading and then applied in the social studies. Objective:

Help the child develop skill in selecting the important point of a paragraph.

Help the child acquire skill in using and understanding the seven color key of a map.

Motor skills include proficiency in manipulative activities such as construction, painting, and drawing. Objective:

Develop the child's skill in the use of a variety of media, including paint, chalk, and charcoal.

Develop his skill in constructing a relief map using plasticene.

Continued practice is essential to ensure increased proficiency of skills.

Practice for some skills is inherent in the social studies while others can be used in any of the subject areas.

A crucial point of any social studies program is the development of a set of effective objectives. Such objectives are related to the purpose, they are understandable to all, and they can be measured by the student's behavior. For instruction to be valuable, the teacher should have a clear idea of how his student's behavior will be affected by his instruction.

Contributions of the Social Sciences

The content of the social studies is derived from the social sciences, which study the actions of humans engaged in the process of living. Each of the social sciences contributes its method of inquiry and its knowledge of human actions. Each of the social sciences (history, geography, political science, economics, sociology, anthropology, psychology, and philosophy) views humans from a different vantage point and uses a unique method of inquiry to acquire its knowledge. What is the vantage point, method of inquiry, and contribution of each social science?

HISTORY

The historian's vantage point is the past. He attempts to obtain a record of human actions. Because he searches for facts that have been preserved, his record is limited to knowledge that has survived. His method of inquiry is basically that of collecting as much data as possible, organizing it, and testing it. In his reconstruction of the facts, the historian interprets them with his own bias within his own frame of reference. Thus, to understand the historian's record of the past, we should know his frame of reference and his bias. His primary purpose is to interpret the present through an understanding of the past and, in so doing, to chart a general course for the future.[6]

The contribution of history is its knowledge of what has happened in the past, which provides meaningful insight into what is happening in the present and what to expect in the future. It is an explanation of the cause and effect relationship of events. Events do not occur in a vacuum —something must have gone before and something will come after. The historian finds what has gone before and suggests what will come after.

[6]John U. Michaelis and A. Montgomery Johnston, eds., *The Social Sciences: Foundations of the Social Studies* (Boston: Allyn & Bacon, Inc., 1965), p. 28.

The contribution of history to the social studies is illustrated by this example. In an attempt to understand why Germany did not become a nation until 1871, we look at her past record of barbarian tribes, constant wars, and provinces ruled by powerful princes. These historical reasons suggest why the unification of these states was delayed.

GEOGRAPHY

The geographer views man in terms of his physical environment and its effect upon his actions. The geographer describes the characteristics of places on the earth, distinguishing one area from another and categorizing them into regions. He is interested in man's activities in these regions to determine whether man is dominated by his environment or has learned to cope with it. In learning to cope with his environment, man—working within his cultural framework—has utilized the available resources and given character to the region.

The geographer's primary method of inquiry is the regional approach, whereby a geographical area is identified "in terms of the specific criteria chosen to delimit it from other regions."[7] The criteria include conditions such as climate, land form, vegetation, manufacturing industries, and internal organization.

Geography's contribution to the social studies is best described by Broek:

The geographer must learn about the biophysical features of the earth; is deeply interested in the interrelations between society and habitat; needs to read the cultural landscape as the earth-engraved expression of man's activity; inspects and compares distributional patterns and formulates concepts and principles.[8]

Applying the geographer's method to the previously stated problem of Germany's late emergence as a nation, we inspect carefully the heavy forests and swamps of the country, which may have formed natural barriers to unification. And we note the existence of few natural boundaries, a fact that might explain Germany's constantly changing national boundaries. These geographical factors may help provide a solution to this problem.

[7]Jan O. M. Broek, *Geography: Its Scope and Spirit* (Columbus, Ohio: Charles E. Merrill Publishing Co., 1965), p. 59.
[8]Broek, *Geography: Its Scope and Spirit*, p. 79.

POLITICAL SCIENCE

Man's attempt to bring order to his life is the concern of the political scientist. He studies man's methods of organizing society in terms of authority at both the family and national level. The political scientist seeks to discover why man extends legitimacy of authority—whether by custom, morality, or legality. He is primarily concerned with the functions and levels of government that extend to all people in society. Political parties, lobbies, and individual powers who provide decision-making policies are of interest to the political scientist.

In recent years, this method of inquiry has become intent upon building a science of political phenomena to express political behavior "in generalizations of theories with explanatory and predictive value."[9] One application of the behaviorists' theory is evident in the study of voting behavior. The behaviorists attempt to discover who votes and why and to generalize from these findings.

Contributing to our knowledge of human actions, the political scientist provides basic information concerning processes, behavior, and institutions of political behavior; political relations among nations; and public policies and ideas about government such as democracy, justice, and equality.[10]

Applying the political scientist's method to Germany's problem, we would seek to determine why Bismarck emerged as a leader capable of unifying a nation. We might ask what influenced the people of the southern German states to vote to become part of a nation under Bismarck's leadership.

ECONOMICS

An economist's concern is leveled at man's ability to adjust his unlimited wants to his limited resources. The economist is interested in man's use of these resources, both human and physical, in producing goods and services and distributing them among people. He seeks to answer questions of what, how, when, and for whom to produce.

Different societies produce different economic systems. "A primary task of economics is to explain both the essential similarities and the nature of the differences in the economic life of different people, so that

[9]David Easton, "Introduction: The Current Meaning of Behavioralism in Political Science," in *The Limits of Behavioralism in Political Science*, ed. James C. Charlesworth (Philadelphia: American Academy of Political Science, 1962), p. 7.

[10]Frank J. Sorauf, *Political Science: an Informal Overview* (Columbus, Ohio: Charles E. Merrill Publishing Co., 1965), p. 7.

man may be better able to understand the conditions under which he lives and the alternatives that are open to him."[11]

If the goals of society (for example, full employment) are not reached, economists attempt to explain this failure and to suggest solutions for fulfillment. Much economic information involves facts and figures, which are measurable and objective. However, the search for answers to economic questions also involves factors such as judgments of conflicting interests and goals, which are immeasurable. The economist contributes knowledge of economic activity in terms of the individual as well as how the system works and the problems encountered.

In analyzing Germany's problem, an economist might consider the diversity of productivity—agricultural, mineral, and industrial—of the many sectors of Germany. Also, he might consider the absence of a good transportation system to bind the country together.

SOCIOLOGY

The interactions of individuals in their associations with one another are of concern to the sociologist. He is interested in man's membership in groups such as the family, school, church, and government. He studies groups—their internal organization, their maintenance processes, and the relations between them. He attempts to determine the influence of these groups upon their members—to recognize the behavioral changes exhibited by them.

The sociologist contributes his knowledge of social institutions (where man has organized in groups). He studies their members, behavior, objectives, norms, roles, values, authority, realia, and location. He describes the social processes, from the simplest interaction to socialization, cooperation, competition, and conflict. He attempts to explain why members of a group behave as they do.

The sociologist is restricted in his inquiry to the information he can observe among and within groups and to that which people are willing to tell him. Many private aspects of human behavior are unavailable to him unless people reveal them through questionnaires, recordings, or interviews.

The life history of Bismarck might be the sociologist's means of explaining the emergence of the German nation. Bismarck's life history, by giving a chronological account of the events of Bismarck's life, would help determine his motives.

---

[11]Richard S. Martin and Rueben G. Miller, *Economics and Its Significance* (Columbus, Ohio: Charles E. Merrill Publishing Company, 1965), p. 9.

ANTHROPOLOGY

The anthropologist views man biologically as he adapts to his environment. These adaptations compose man's culture—his customs, laws, beliefs, physical characteristics, and language. Anthropology is primarily concerned with non-Western cultures, although there is increased interest in the study of complex modern societies such as the United States and Europe. Anthropological study involves searching for the artifacts of early cultures, attempting to date their existence, and trying to formulate an understanding of their structure and general characteristics, as well as learning about cultures as they exist today.

Methods of inquiry employed by the anthropologist include field study, whether it is archaeological digging for remains of early people or living with people whose present culture is being studied. The anthropologist analyzes and classifies the information he collects. Thus, extensive knowledge about the culture of man is provided—knowledge of sources of words in language, physical attributes of different races, customs of marriage and religion, and behavior patterns of members of the cultures.

In studying Germany's situation, anthropologists would certainly attempt to identify aspects of German culture that might be responsible for Germany's late unification. They might investigate the different peoples of the north and south regions.

PSYCHOLOGY AND PHILOSOPHY

Only recently have psychology and philosophy been included in the social studies, and their contributions are not as well established as are those of the other social sciences.

Psychology is man's attempt to understand himself and the actions of those around him. It seeks to discover the cause-effect relationships of human behavior and, thus, to make predictions about future behavior. Generally, the inquiry is directed toward individuals or small groups.

Philosophy is the seeking and accumulating of truths about reality, value, logic, and knowledge. It has been called the mother of the other sciences—as the individual areas of knowledge increased, they separated from the parent. Philosophy is broad and inclusive. It has been described as "an attempt to discover the whole truth about everything."[12]

Throughout the preceding discussion of the contributions of the social sciences, the tremendous overlapping of the areas of concern is obvious. As a result of this overlapping, combinations of the sciences appear such

[12]Michaelis *et al.*, eds., *The Social Sciences: Foundations of the Social Studies*, p. 243.

as social psychology, cultural geography, political sociology, cultural history, and economic geography.

Because the social sciences are concerned with human actions, each contributes its knowledge of these actions to the other disciplines. The composite of their knowledge provides the foundation for the social studies.

SELECTED REFERENCES

Clements, H. Millard, William R. Fielder, and B. Robert Tabachnick, *Social Study: Inquiry in Elementary Classrooms*. Indianapolis: The Bobbs-Merrill Company, Inc., 1966.

Douglass, Malcolm P., *Social Studies From Theory to Practice in Elementary Education*. Philadelphia: J. B. Lippincott Co., 1967.

Dunfee, Maxine and Helen Sagl, *Social Studies Through Problem Solving*. New York: Holt, Rinehart & Winston, Inc., 1966.

Estvan, Frank, *Social Studies in a Changing World*. New York: Harcourt, Brace & World, Inc., 1968.

Fraser, Dorothy and Samuel P. McCutchen, eds., *Social Studies in Transition: Guidelines for Change*. Washington, D.C.: National Council for the Social Studies, 1965.

Gibson, John S., *New Frontiers in the Social Studies: Action and Analysis*. New York: Citation Press, 1967.

Jarolimek, John, *Social Studies in Elementary Education* (second ed.). New York: The Macmillan Company, 1967.

Michaelis, John U., *Social Studies for Children in a Democracy, Recent Trends and Developments* (fourth ed.). Englewood Cliffs, N.J.: Prentice-Hall, Inc., 1968.

Michaelis, John U. and A. Montgomery Johnston, eds., *The Social Sciences: Foundations of the Social Studies*. Boston: Allyn & Bacon, Inc., 1965.

Muessig, Raymond H. and Vincent R. Rogers, eds., *Social Science Seminar Series*. Columbus, Ohio: Charles E. Merrill Publishing Co., 1965.

Ragan, William B. and John D. McAulay, *Social Studies for Today's Children*. New York: Appleton-Century-Crofts, Inc., 1964.

CHAPTER TWO

Social Studies Curriculum Development

SOCIAL STUDIES CURRICULUMS FOR ELEMENTARY SCHOOL ARE developed by a number of agencies, which are found at local, state, and national levels. A teacher's social studies program should be based on the needs and interests of the children in his classroom; however, it is directed by guidelines established for the local school district, state requirements, and general trends advocated by national agencies such as the U.S. Office of Education and the National Council for the Social Studies.

During the last decade, a battle has raged over the method of teaching and the content involved in social studies programs in the elementary school. The expanding horizons or environment theory established by Paul R. Hanna dominated the organization and content of the social studies for many years. This theory advocates that the child should first study the environment around him in terms of basic human activities. For example, in kinder-

FIGURE 1. Individual classroom instruction is based on the needs and interests of the children and is directed by local school guidelines, state requirements, and national trends.

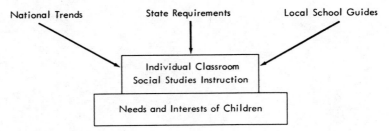

garten or first grade, the child learns of the activities of the family and home. In second grade, his environment is expanded to the school and local community. Successively, throughout the remainder of the elementary grades, the child is introduced to the broader community, state, nation, western hemisphere, and world. The theory contends that, initially, a child understands best the environment that is most familiar to him. The curriculum content centers around the human activities involved in production, communication, government, transportation, protection, creation, religion, recreation, education, and the expression of aesthetic impulses.

Many conditions in our society have been responsible for suggested alterations in this theory. Frequently, educators focus attention upon the advent of Sputnik as the impetus for radical changes in our educational programs. In the area of social studies, however, failure to point out conditions that initiated change previous to Sputnik would be unfortunate.

For example, the position of the United States as a world leader following World War Two placed greater strain on the social studies to prepare citizens to accept this tremendous responsibility. No longer is the United States permitted to isolate itself without concern for what is happening in the rest of the world.

Equally important in the development of new educational programs is the emergence of underdeveloped nations seeking a place in the diplomatic world. Nations that were infrequently included in the social studies curriculum such as China, Egypt, and the African countries must now be a part of the study so that understanding of their positions can be accomplished.

The strain of international relations in the cold war between the communist and noncommunist countries necessitates a more thorough study of ideologies. Also, more understanding of our American heritage is necessary to provide a basis for comparison.

Ease of transportation, which permits more travel and contact of peoples from around the world, places pressure on the social studies to provide understanding of different cultures. The mobility of people into our communities from other countries adds emphasis to this task.

Educators such as Jerrold R. Zacharias and Jerome Bruner have influenced the social studies curriculum with their research and development programs, which stress the structure of the disciplines and a major change in the theory of instruction. Social studies, however, has been one of the last areas to be affected by these programs.

Project Social Studies, which was initiated by the U. S. Office of Education in 1962 to encourage social scientists and educators to develop new programs, adds its pressure to social studies education. These new programs emphasize the inclusion and extension in elementary social studies of content from all of the social sciences. The impact of these programs is now being realized at most levels.

Federal monies that placed emphasis on educating the culturally disadvantaged resulted in the development of programs and materials for these students. A natural outcome of this emphasis on individual differences was the establishment of programs for students of exceptional ability.

More recently, pressures within our society have influenced the teaching of social studies. The rapid urbanization of our nation has changed the living patterns of people. The close contact of people in an urbanized society requires the development of better human relationships and an understanding of the problems created by our crowded cities. Technological advancements also have had their effect. Limited working hours provide more leisure time, which should be channeled toward worthwhile endeavors. Mechanization has virtually eliminated pride in craftsmanship and has created a need for some replacement for this reward. Pressures created by the social and racial problems in our society present a real challenge to the social studies. Content that depicted a picture of the white middle-class American does not suffice in a world that knows extensive poverty and men of all colors.

The previously discussed conditions have resulted in fervent attempts to initiate changes in social studies education. A discussion of the programs developed by agencies at local, state, and national levels will explain the tremendous divergency of programs currently in existence.

Local

Development of social studies programs at the local level is generally the responsibility of committees of teachers, curriculum specialists, or administrators. Frequently, assistance is solicited from local colleges and universities or the state department.

The type of social studies program established by a local school district results from studies of the conditions inherent in the school environment. The following conditions are examined to help determine the social studies program to be adopted by the district: community environment, socioeconomic level of the students, experiential background of the students, aspiration level of the students, general educational goals of the school, and materials available.

COMMUNITY ENVIRONMENT, SOCIOECONOMIC LEVEL, AND EXPERIENTIAL BACKGROUND

Environmental factors influence the type of social studies program that is introduced into a school system—a meaningful series of learning experiences for children in a rural area would not necessarily prove as fruitful for children in an urban community or in an affluent suburban district. The reason for this variation obviously lies in the everyday experiences of each group of children. Many of the situations confronting the children in the city, the suburbs, and the rural areas would differ greatly.

The socioeconomic level of the children in each area also affects their experiential background. The child from an affluent suburban home may have traveled extensively, been exposed to an enriching vocabulary, and been surrounded by books, magazines, and newspapers. The urban child from a poverty area may have traveled no more than four blocks from home, never seen books until entering school, and received little direct communication from adults. Because they bring such different experiential backgrounds to the school situation, the children from these two environments certainly should not be confronted with the same social studies experiences. Children with rich experiential backgrounds benefit from a program that builds upon their experiences and expands their horizons. They are able to handle more abstract material. In comparison, children with a paucity of experiences need a program molded to provide the experiences lacking in their backgrounds. A major portion of such a program would include field trips, a wealth of visual materials (such as pictures, films, filmstrips, books, and magazines), enriching cultural activities, and concrete experiences for vocabulary development. Obviously, programs for both areas would contain certain basic elements, although they would vary in their approach and content.

Large school districts with varying environmental areas within their boundaries may find it necessary to adopt several social studies programs to meet the needs of their children from divergent backgrounds.

INTELLIGENCE AND ASPIRATION LEVEL OF STUDENTS

Home, community, and school environments play an important role in the intelligence and aspiration levels children achieve. Studies conclude that socioeconomic factors influence the intelligence level of children—those from lower-socioeconomic levels score significantly lower on intelligence tests than those from middle-socioeconomic levels.[1] School achievement is apparently related to socioeconomic status as well.[2] The aspiration level is also affected by the amount of motivation, interest, and support children receive from their environments, which include the home, the peer group, and the school. Obviously, social studies program planning should be influenced by these factors.

Children with apparent lower intelligence and aspiration levels need enriching experiences to stimulate their interest in learning and increase their motivation for achievement. For example, children from minority groups would benefit from the inclusion in their social studies programs of studies of the history and contribution of their groups to our national heritage.

The above average in intelligence should be challenged by more depth studies of topics and extensive use of their creative ability and initiative in completing work; the quality of their work should be expected to be higher; they should be provided with material that will interest and excite them on their intellectual level; and they should acquire skills that will prepare them for an advanced education. An important attitude for the superior student to acquire is one of respect for his ability plus respect and appreciation for the contributions of those of lesser ability.

EDUCATIONAL GOALS OF THE SCHOOL

The social studies program planned by the local school district should certainly contribute to the overall goals of the elementary school. If the school's intent is to help each child develop to the extent of his potential

[1]Martin Deutsch and M. Brown, "Social Influence in Negro-White Intelligence Differences," *Journal of Social Issues*, XX (December, 1964), 24–35.

[2]E. H. Hill and M. C. Giammatteo, "Socio-Economic Status and Its Relationship to School Achievement in the Elementary School," *Elementary English*, XL (March, 1963), 265–70.

in order that he may become an effective member of society, the social studies program should accept the responsibility of helping the student develop skill in and an understanding of human relationships.

MATERIALS

The extent of materials necessary to make a program effective should be considered before the program is developed. Some programs require extensive libraries, resource materials, audio-visual aids, and artifacts that may not be available in some districts. However, often-overlooked community resources such as the museum, public library, and speakers can add considerably to the limited resources of a school district.

OTHER FACTORS AFFECTING LOCAL SCHOOL PROGRAMS

Local school programs are also affected by state requirements, which may control both content and materials. Certain states have adopted laws that require the inclusion of topics such as American Heritage or Principles of Communism. Other states have designated specific textbooks that must be used by the schools.

National trends advocated by social studies educators, the U. S. Office of Education, and the National Council for the Social Studies frequently influence the programs of local agencies. Often, school districts are requested to field test programs developed by these national agencies.

An example of a social studies program developed by a local school district is the Plymouth and Whitemarsh Social Studies Course of Study. It consists of illustrative units provided for each elementary grade level. The program is based on the following philosophy:

PHILOSOPHY OF THE SOCIAL STUDIES DEPARTMENT

History indicates that those nations which have contributed most to the development of man are those that have profited by a careful analysis of their heritage. The main objective of the academic disciplines within the social studies should be to examine our historical legacy and use it as a guide to the present as well as a blueprint for the future. It therefore behooves us as social studies teachers to enlighten our students who are entering society by exposing them to the following concepts:

1. That a dominant factor in this contemporary period of history is an outgoing and accelerating scientific and social revolution.
2. That basic changes in American life should be viewed in relation to the traditional values of our free society.

3. That we must maintain our freedom to solve our problems according to established American ideas and ideals.

4. That the progress that society makes will depend largely on the ability of the individuals within that society to comprehend these changes and adapt themselves accordingly.

5. That geographic environment has a profound effect on man's institutions and ways of living.

6. That social studies should aid in the development of an informed, responsible, and effective citizenship.

7. That we should encourage open discussion of those issues involved in the maintenance of a free society.

8. That we should attempt to create within individuals a widening knowledge and understanding in an ever-growing interdependent world.

9. That we should make students aware of those moral and ethical standards which contribute to their effectiveness as human beings.

   With all the emphasis in today's society on the physical sciences, one truth emerges—science has indeed given the world proximity, but it has not given it community. World community can come only from an understanding of and appreciation for the varied societies which make up our world; and this can be achieved through the social sciences.[3]

The scope and sequence of the program follow:

SCOPE AND SEQUENCE CHART

	KINDERGARTEN	GRADE 1	GRADE 2
Our American Heritage	Heroes & Holidays	Heroes, Holidays & Loyalty Current Events	Heroes, Holidays & Loyalty Current Events
Man's Economic Needs	Child's Immediate Environment	Our Homes, Families, Farms, and Schools	Our Community & Township & Its Services, Cities, & Suburbs
Our Nation's Interdependence with Other Nations	Learning to Live in a Group	Finding Out About Maps and Globes	Reading Maps of our Township, Pennsylvania, and the U. S. Map and Globe Skills
Empathy With Other Cultures	Respecting Other Social Backgrounds	Homes, Families, & Farms Around the World	Villages, Towns, and Cities Around the World

[3]*Elementary Social Studies Course of Study, Plymouth and Whitemarsh Public Schools* (Pennsylvania: Plymouth Meeting, 1964).

SCOPE AND SEQUENCE CHART (*continued*)

GRADE 3	GRADE 4	GRADE 5	GRADE 6
Famous Countians and Pennsylvanians Contributions of Pennsylvanians to U.S.	How Man Lived and Existed Development of Community and City Living	America's Economic Growth	How Peoples Around the World Earn their Livings
Geography of Our State Map and Globe Skills	Fundamentals of Geography SRA Map and Globe Skills	Geography of United States, Canada, and South America SRA Map and Graph Skills Foreign Settlement of America	SRA Reporting and Outlining Skills Steps in Map Reading The Geography and Cultures of Peoples and Nations Around the World
Foreign Culture Contributions to State and County	Beginnings of the Cultural Patterns of the Nations Under Study	The American Culture	The Geography and Cultures of Peoples and Nations Around the World[4]

A sample unit from first grade is *Families Around the World*. The aims listed for the unit are:

FAMILIES AROUND THE WORLD—FIRST GRADE

I. Aims

A. To understand that the family is the oldest human institution and in many ways it is the most important.

B. To realize that it is society's most basic unit.

C. To appreciate that entire civilizations have survived or disappeared, depending on whether family life was strong or weak.

D. To understand that families serve three vital human needs:
1. The means for producing children and continuing the human race.
2. Provide for the protections and early training of infants.
3. Set up a division of labor so that each member contributes something.

E. To understand that family life is the same in all parts of the world, but, in other ways, it differs from country to country and even from section to section.[5]

[4]*Elementary Social Studies Course of Study. Ibid.*
[5]*Elementary Social Studies Course of Study. Ibid.*

Suggested content for the unit is included:

II. Content

A. Marriage

1. Legal contract to live together as husband and wife.
2. Legal responsibility to support and care for any children they may have.
3. A successful marriage is a happy one.
4. Different forms (For teacher's information).
   a. Most societies practice monogamy (marriage of one man and one woman).
   b. A few allow polygamy (more than one mate). (Marriage of a man with more than one woman at a time, called polygyny, is more common than polyandry, in which a woman marries more than one man at a time.)

B. Home Life

1. Caring for the children.
2. Preparing meals.
3. Eating together.
4. Keeping house.
5. Playing games.
6. Entertaining friends.
7. Influenced by way family is organized.
   a. Patriarchal (most families throughout human history).
      (1) The father heads the family.
      (2) The woman takes her husband's name.
      (3) Children bear their father's name.
   b. Matriarchal (a few societies).
      (1) Mother heads family.
      (2) Husband lives with wife's family.
      (3) Women own property and pass it on to daughters.
   c. Equalitarian (Western nations).
      (1) Each member is respected and no one tries to be "boss."
      (2) Mother and father share responsibility.
      (3) Children can express their opinions and have a good deal of freedom in family.
      (4) "Council meetings" to make important decisions.
      (5) Most common in United States, Canada, and Western Europe.

C. Responsibilities

1. Legal
   a. Support their children.

        b. No physical or mental harm to each other.

        c. Laws impose punishment for neglect or abuse.

     2. Respect and help each other.

        a. Cooperation.

        b. Parents have responsibility of protecting and caring for their children and of gradually teaching them to care for themselves.

D. Problems

     1. Not earning enough money.

     2. Mother being ill.

     3. Parents quarreling.

     4. A child rebelling and becoming hard to handle.

     5. Childless homes.

     6. Unhappiness may end in divorce (Family life breaks down).

        a. Consult a physician, a religious leader, or a trained family counselor.

        b. Government and religious agencies.

E. Family Relationships

     1. Relatives

        a. Blood—through birth (aunts, uncles, cousins, grandparents, etc.).

        b. Affinity—through marriage (in-laws).

        c. Laws regulate marriage between relatives.

     2. Family Trees

        a. Charts that show the earliest known ancestor of a family and all the persons who are descended from him.

        b. Family crests and coats of arms.

        c. Hand down traditional names or mottoes.

        d. Some own precious heirlooms.

F. Family Life Around the World

     1. Brazil

     2. Denmark

     3. England

     4. India

     5. Russia

G. History

     1. Joint family (all living descendants).

        a. Self-sufficient.

        b. Cooperative.

     2. Clans (several joint families).

        a. Banded together.

        b. Shared certain ceremonies and traditions.

3. Tribes (several clans living in same territory and sharing the same culture).
   a. Self-governing.
   b. Protected members against attacks from wild animals and enemy tribes.
4. States
5. Nations
6. Industrial Revolution
   a. Workers moved away from local communities and kinship groupings in order to be near jobs.
   b. Nuclear families consisting of married couple and children broke down joint families.
7. Families depend more on love and companionship than on blood relationships today.[6]

The activities for the unit attempt to take into consideration the interests and background of the children in the class.

III. Activities

A. Initiating
   1. Display pictures of families from around the world and discuss differences in their appearance and dress.
   2. Discuss various forms of family fun and recreation among families.

B. Correlating
   1. Discuss family members and make charts about the roles of the various members.
   2. Read stories about families around the world.
   3. Learn games that children and families play from around the world.
   4. Discuss various family customs and traditions of families in the class.
   5. Share samples of holiday foods from different religious backgrounds of the children in the class.
   6. Draw pictures of the way families have fun in faraway places.
   7. Dress dolls or stick puppets according to other countries around the world.

C. Culminating
   1. Display of costumed dolls.

[6]*Elementary Social Studies Course of Study. Ibid.*

2. Draw pictures to be pasted on a TV "tape" and class may write
   a script.[7]

State

Responsibility for social studies curriculum development at the state
level generally rests with the curriculum specialists of the state departments, often with assistance from public school personnel and university
and college professors of social science and education. State departments
establish broad guidelines for local districts, interpret state laws, and
provide leadership for initiating change within the existing programs.

Previously, state departments issued curriculum bulletins that were
followed religiously. Deviations from the established program were not
encouraged and few opportunities for creative teaching were possible.
In addition, adjustments necessary to provide meaningful programs
adapted to local needs were lacking. Now, however, a trend toward
more flexibility in the use of these bulletins is apparent; generally, they
are used as guides to instructional programs. The establishment of broad
guidelines from the state departments gives the needed direction and
continuity to the local programs, but permits the variations necessary
for adaptation to local situations.

State requirements established by the legislature are interpreted to the
local districts by the state departments. Frequently, they are also responsible for establishing programs to implement state requirements. In states
where textbooks are adopted on a statewide basis, it is the responsibility
of the textbook committee of the state department to make these selections. Thus, the type of text materials to be utilized by the districts is
often a state responsibility.

By using its guidelines and considering national trends, the state department can evaluate current programs more objectively than can local
departments. The Oregon Council for Curriculum and Instruction, for
example, has developed a project whereby the state is divided into ten
regional districts for pre-evaluation of the current programs before insti-
tuting any major revisions.[8]

Leadership for introducing change in the social studies curriculum
should be provided at the state level. Certain states have been more

---

[7]*Elementary Social Studies Course of Study. Ibid.*
[8]John S. Gibson, *New Frontiers in the Social Studies* (New York: Citation Press,
1967), p. 49.

active in this respect than others. The state departments of Wisconsin, Minnesota, Indiana, California, New York, and Connecticut are among those that have either organized or encouraged curriculum revisions.[9] A more detailed look at the Wisconsin program will provide opportunity for a comparison of the programs developed at local and state levels.

A Conceptual Framework for the Social Studies in Wisconsin Schools was the result of collaboration between the Wisconsin Social Studies Committee and research scholars from colleges and universities. The bulletin's introduction gives an explanation of its basic philosophy:

Factual knowledge is one aspect of the curriculum that most teachers recognize, teach, and test. Until recently most teachers, consciously or otherwise, have accepted the idea of the existence of a body of "conventional wisdom." This information answered the question "What should be known?" or "What should be taught?" Such a viewpoint is incomplete. While much of the knowledge that has stood the test of time will continue to merit consideration, much new, vital information has been generated. Not all facts can or should be learned; furthermore, these fragments of information often have little relevance in themselves. To resolve this problem, teachers should help students to collect and organize into concepts the multiplicity of facts that confront them.[10]

The bulletin contains introductory statements concerning the disciplines, history, geography, anthropology-sociology, economics, and political science. It also offers generalizations incorporating major concepts of each discipline and topic variants for each discipline for grades kindergarten through 12. Suggested use of the bulletin by teachers is identified thus:

The pages within this bulletin attempt to demonstrate how the course content at each grade level can be used to develop these concepts and generalizations in a spiralling manner from kindergarten through the 12th grade. By following any strand, the reader will note that the developmental variants emerge in greater depth and sophistication at each succeeding grade level.

This bulletin suggests the interrelated nature of history, geography, and the social sciences. An "orchestration" of these areas is implied in the developmental variants which appear at each grade level. This approach would encourage the teacher and students to draw against the concepts and structure of the several social studies areas in the consideration of any topic or problem.

It is not intended that the statements of the basic concepts nor the variants will be taught as items to be committed to memory but rather as illuminating

[9]Gibson, *New Frontiers in the Social Studies*, p. 49.

[10]*A Conceptual Framework for the Social Studies in Wisconsin Schools*, rev. ed. (Madison, Wisconsin: Wisconsin State Department of Education, 1967), p. 2.

ideas or analytic generalizations which will emerge from what has been studied. Care should be taken that the concepts *do* emerge and then are applied to new situations. Mere verbalization of rules or masses of information is not effective social studies education. Students should be helped to acquire meaning by use of the common elements presented. As students use the conceptual strands they should be given new challenges and presented with opportunities to see new applications at even higher levels until they gain the habit of arriving at valid analyses and generalizations of their own.[11]

Topics introduced at each grade level include:

Kindergarten: Home and School
Grade one: Home, School, Neighborhood
Grade two: Community Life
Grade three: Community Life in Other Lands
Grade four: Wisconsin
Grade five: United States Geography and History
Grade six: Selected Cultures (Food Gathering, Agrarian Handicraft, and Industrial Complexes)
Grade seven: Man in His Political World
Grade eight: Western Civilization
Grade nine: Area Studies (Non-Western)
Grade ten: United States History to 1896
Grade eleven: United States History, 1896 to Present
Grade twelve: Advanced Courses in History, Problems and the Social Sciences

Selected major concepts from each discipline and the developmental variants for United States Geography and History in grade 5 are reproduced on p. 31 to supply an understanding of the nature of this bulletin.

National

At the national level there are a number of agencies that are involved in curriculum development, many of which influence social studies education. For a number of years, the National Council for the Social Studies, a department of the National Education Association, has devoted itself to the improvement of social studies education. *Social Education*, the official journal of the organization, provides information representing the

[11]*Conceptual Framework for the Social Studies*, p. 3.

GENERALIZATIONS INCORPORATING MAJOR SOCIAL STUDIES CONCEPTS

HISTORY	ANTHROPOLOGY-SOCIOLOGY	POLITICAL SCIENCE	ECONOMICS	GEOGRAPHY
Change is inevitable, and the rate of change is uneven among and within societies.	Man is a unique being, and while each individual is unique in some ways, greater similarities exist among men than dissimilarities.	Every society creates laws. Penalties and sanctions are provided for violations of law.	The conflict between unlimited wants and limited natural and human resources is the basic economic problem. Scarcity still persists in the world today.	Spatial relationship exists between any place on earth and all other places. A relationship between two or more locations involves direction, distance, and time.

DEVELOPMENTAL VARIANTS

HISTORY	ANTHROPOLOGY-SOCIOLOGY	POLITICAL SCIENCE	ECONOMICS	GEOGRAPHY
The people of the United States have met their problems with varying degrees of success.	The United States today has the natural resources and technical know-how to meet the basic needs of most of its people.	The Constitution is the supreme law of the land—it gives Congress the power to enact national laws.	While abundant natural resources alone do not insure a high standard of living, unequal distribution of natural resources has been a contributing factor to "pockets of poverty" in all stages of American development.	The United States occupies a uniquely located part of the rotating spherical earth and is related to all other nations in terms of size, distance, direction, and time.[12]

[12]*Conceptual Framework for the Social Studies*, pp. 20, 21.

current thinking in social studies. Its yearbook and other publications pinpoint problem areas in social studies and supply needed guidance and material to aid in their solution.

The National Council for Geographic Education, through the *Journal of Geography*, and the American Historical Association expend considerable effort toward improving the teaching of their respective disciplines in the elementary school. Both provide leadership and materials to stimulate interest in and concern for social studies education.

The Joint Council in Economic Education is an example of a national group committed to the improvement of economic education. In 1964, the group initiated a project entitled "Developmental Economic Education Program" (DEEP). The three major objectives of this project are "(1) to build economic understandings into school curricula, (2) to improve teacher education in economics, and (3) to develop and test new teaching materials at all grade levels."[13] DEEP supplies a variety of materials for students in grades 1 through 12, a teacher training program via television, and clearing house services for economic materials.

By means of its financial assistance to Project Social Studies, a part of the Cooperative Research Program initiated in 1962, the United States Office of Education has supplied a major impetus for curriculum change in the social studies. These projects, initiated at major colleges and universities across the nation and involving social scientists and educators, have approached change from a variety of viewpoints. For example, Roy Price, of Syracuse University, sought to identify major social science concepts and to utilize them in developing instructional materials. John Michaelis, of the University of California, prepared teaching guides and materials on the Asian Countries for grades 1–12. New approaches and materials for a sequential curriculum on American society for grades 5–12 became the concern of John Lee, of Northwestern University. Charlotte Crabtree, of the University of California at Los Angeles, was involved with teaching geography in grades 1–3.

One of the most widely acclaimed projects, titled "Development of a Sequential Curriculum in Anthropology for Grades 1–7," was instituted at the University of Georgia by Wilfred Bailey and Marion Rice. A more than cursory look at the rationale and content of this project will be presented to further underline the diversity of programs conceived at the local, state, and national level.

The Anthropology Project was a cooperative venture involving members of the Department of Sociology and Anthropology and the College of Education. The rationale of the project is based upon these premises:

[13]Gibson, *New Frontiers in the Social Studies*, p. 96.

1. Any field of knowledge, such as anthropology, consists of a system of symbols, or word labels, which are used to express ideas and describe relationships. An understanding or mastery of any field of knowledge begins with an understanding of the symbol system, the meaning of which expands and develops as the knowledge of the discipline is extended.

2. Symbol systems are usually organized for transmission of a core of congruent ideas, usually referred to as subject matter, discipline, or field. For almost thirty years, the social studies movement has contended that a subject approach to the transmission of social studies is inappropriate for the elementary grades. It is thought that any type of organization of material, irrespective of its method, is designed to transmit knowledge, and there is nothing incompatible, except preference and tradition, with a subject presentation of a social science in the elementary grades.

3. Anthropological material is frequently used in the public school, but, in the absence of emphasis on anthropological concepts and terminology, the contribution that anthropology has to make to an understanding of man and of different cultures is frequently obscured. The material deliberately introduces anthropological terminology which may at first be somewhat difficult for the student. As his familiarity with these terms increases, however, it is expected that they will help him to organize and interpret in a more meaningful manner the world in which he lives.[14]

Organization of the program follows a cyclical pattern, with concepts developed in the primary cycle repeated and enlarged in the intermediate cycle. The Concept of Culture is the topic presented for grades 1 and 4. In grade 1, three ethnographies—the American, Kazak, and Aruntas—are presented through oral discussion by the teacher and a picture text for the children. The comparison cultures of Kazak and Aruntas were chosen because they would be little known by teacher and pupil, and stereotypes of them would not have been established. Grade 4 develops the same topic; however, it emphasizes a more analytical approach with the organizing of cultural constructs.

The Development of Man and His Culture is the topic presented for grades 2 and 5. Units on New World Prehistory for grade 2 and Old World Prehistory for grade 5 are provided. The objective of the unit for grade 2 is to provide a background for understanding man and his culture, emphasizing the following fundamental principles:

1. Archaeologists use definite and orderly methods in studying the past. These are: (a) archaeological sites are located and classified; (b) archaeological

---

[14]*The Development of Man and His Culture*, No. 30 (Athens, Georgia: Anthropology Curriculum Project, University of Georgia, 1966), pp. 1–2.

sites are carefully excavated using the proper tools and techniques; (c) archaeological sites are dated using either relative or absolute dating methods; (d) the results of an archaeological excavation are interpreted and published.

2. Archaeological excavation can recover only a part of the past.

3. The entrance and development of man in the New World followed a certain sequence. This was: (a) Man entered the New World as *Homo sapiens*, at least 10,000 years ago, following or hunting for large game animals by way of the Bering Straits; (b) American Indians developed various stages of culture; (c) these states of culture were not in the order of a developmental sequence except in Nuclear America.[15]

The teacher's guide to New World Prehistory suggests procedures for teaching the unit. The sequence of events includes a pre-test to establish the students' achievement levels; the teaching of sections on Archaeological Methods, New World Prehistory, and Hopi Indians; a summary and review; and a post-test. The unit requires approximately twenty-six days of one-hour periods, and the guide suggests that it can be taught to replace another social studies unit.

Objectives, content, activities, review questions, bibliography, and a vocabulary glossary for each area of study are provided in the guide. A background material booklet for teachers and a text and guide for pupils are included in the materials.

Chapter one of the pupil's text begins as follows:

ARCHAEOLOGICAL METHODS

1. An Archaeologist at Work

Archaeology is the study of how man lived long ago. Scientists who study how man lived long ago are called *archaeologists*.

An *archaeologist* studies artifacts. *Artifacts* are things made by man. Everything that man makes is called an *artifact*. Pots, spearheads, houses, and clothing are examples of artifacts. *Artifacts* are found where man lived, worked, or hunted long ago. An archaeologist learns how man lived long ago from *artifacts*.[16]

Activities suggested for this section include taking a museum field trip, building a terrarium showing stratification, building a frieze illustrating steps in making an archaeological excavation, and arranging a display

---

[15]*The Development of Man and His Culture*, No. 30, pp. 1–2.
[16]*The Development of Man and His Culture: New World Prehistory*, No. 28 (Athens, Georgia: Anthropology Curriculum Project, University of Georgia, 1966), p. 1.

of the tools of the archaeologist. Review questions formulated for this section are:

1. Suppose you had gone camping recently. Would someone in the future be able to tell that you had camped there? Why or why not?
2. What type of artifacts might our culture leave behind for archaeologists of the future to find?
3. Which type of site would tell you most about a culture of the past, a habitation site or a chipping station? Explain.
4. Which type of date would be the best to have, a relative date or an absolute date? Why?
5. Do you think a carefully made piece of pottery found near the surface of the ground was probably made at a latter date than a roughly made arrowhead found deep in the ground? Explain.
6. Why is it necessary for an archaeologist to make a careful record of what he finds?[17]

A project such as the Anthropology Project stresses the importance of social science content beyond the usual history and geography for children in the elementary school. It also stresses the value in helping the children behave as social scientists, learning their method of inquiry and attempting to study the problems of society.

Agencies at each of the levels—local, state, and national—provide social studies programs that represent their interpretations of what should compose social studies education. An analysis of the examples from each level reiterates the presence of the quite divergent programs to be adopted by school districts.

The local school system can provide specific objectives and a more detailed presentation of its program based on the needs and interests of its children. State programs are broad and general, indicating a framework from which the local school districts can build their curriculum guides. National programs for curriculum development exemplify the current thinking of educators and social scientists. National programs are designed to provide exacting information and guidance for teachers and children. Their goal is to affect the curriculum development of the local and state agencies.

SELECTED REFERENCES

Bailey, Wilfred and Marion Rice, *Anthropology Curriculum Project*. Athens, Georgia: University of Georgia, 1966.

[17]*The Development of Man and His Culture*, No. 30, pp. 11–12.

Chase, W. Linwood, *A Guide for the Elementary Social Studies Teacher.* Boston: Allyn & Bacon, Inc., 1966.

Conceptual Framework: Social Studies. Madison: Wisconsin State Department of Education, 1967.

Gibson, John S., *New Frontiers in the Social Studies: Goals for Students, Means for Teachers.* New York: Citation Press, 1967.

Goodlad, John, *The Changing School Curriculum.* New York: Fund for the Advancement of Education, 1966.

Massialas, Byron G. and Frederick R. Smith, eds., *New Challenges in the Social Studies.* Belmont, Calif.: Wadsworth Publishing Co., Inc., 1965.

Muessig, Raymond H., *Social Studies Curriculum Improvement: A Guide for Local Committees,* Bulletin No. 36. Washington, D.C.: National Council for the Social Studies, 1965.

Social Studies Framework for the Public Schools of California. Sacramento, Calif.: California State Department of Education, 1967.

Taba, Hilda, *Teachers' Handbook for Elementary Social Studies.* Reading, Mass.: Addison-Wesley Publishing Co., Inc., 1967.

What methods of teaching social studies should be used with children?

PART TWO

Methodology

ALTHOUGH TEXTBOOKS AND STATE AND LOCAL CURRICULUM guides are provided for teachers, a teacher must ultimately design a social studies program to meet the needs of the children in his classroom. What method of approach will he use? Method is defined as the procedures followed in achieving the goals of the social studies program. For example, should children learn to solve problems through the method of inquiry? Should children learn social science concepts by studying the structure of the discipline? Should children learn to think and behave as social scientists? Do disadvantaged children learn most effectively through concrete experiences? Should a variety of approaches be used throughout the year?

This section will discuss several methods of approach: (1) problem solving through inquiry, (2) unit development, (3) method derived from the structure of the social science disciplines, and (4) method for the disadvantaged child.

Each discussion will include a definition of the method and an explanation of the objectives, philosophy, selection of content, and organization of the program, with an appropriate example. Also included and equally important will be a comparison of the advantages and disadvantages of each method.

CHAPTER THREE

Problem Solving Through Inquiry

THE METHOD OF TEACHING PROBLEM SOLVING THROUGH inquiry has often been misunderstood and misused because of discrepancies in the definitions given for the terms "problem solving," "inquiry," "reflective thinking," "inductive reasoning," and "discovery." Frequently, these terms are used interchangeably without explanation of their different meanings.

Problem solving is the process whereby an individual identifies a problem situation, formulates tentative explanations or hypotheses, verifies these tentative hypotheses by gathering and evaluating data, and restates the hypotheses or arrives at generalizations. The individual may then apply these generalizations to new situations.

Many authors use reflective thinking and inductive reasoning to identify the problem-solving method. Early in the thirties, Dewey referred to the identification of the problem as the prereflective period, to the search for an answer as the reflective period, and to the dispelling of doubt as the postreflective period.[1]

Inductive reasoning or inductive teaching is described as the process of leading an individual toward solving a problem by providing him with sufficient stimulation and a direction based on hypotheses.

In contrast, inquiry is the method of searching for the solution to a problem.

Inquiry is not conducted as an indiscriminant search for facts; it is instead, an organized, directed search.[2]

Hypotheses direct its activities . . . Hypotheses determine what facts will be selected as relevant to the problem. They influence what interpretations are formulated and accepted in the end.[3]

Discovery may occur as the individual is conducting his search—he reassembles or reorganizes information based on previous and newly acquired learning and gains insight into the problem.

Bruner states that discovery

. . . is in its essence a matter of rearranging or transforming evidence in such a way that one is enabled to go beyond the evidence so reassembled to new insights. It may well be that an additional fact or shred of evidence makes this larger transformation possible. But it is often not even dependent on new information.[4]

Therefore, inquiry and discovery can be defined as steps in the problem-solving process.

The problem-solving approach in teaching rests solidly on the ability of children to think effectively. Taba relates, "The task of instruction is to provide systematic training in thinking and to help students acquire cognitive skills which are necessary for thinking autonomously and productively."[5] There is a sequential order, as Piaget shows, in the development of forms of thought from childhood to adulthood; each step is a prerequisite to the next. A student should manipulate concrete

[1]John Dewey, *How We Think* (Boston: D. C. Heath and Company, 1933), p. 106.

[2]Joseph J. Schwab, *The Teaching of Science as Inquiry* (Cambridge: Harvard University Press, 1962), p. 14, cited in Charlotte Crabtree, "Supporting Reflective Thinking in the Classroom," in *Effective Thinking in The Social Studies*, eds. Jean Fair and Fannie Shaftel (Washington, D.C.: National Council for the Social Studies, 1967), p. 89.

[3]Fair and Shaftel, eds., *Effective Thinking*, p. 89.

[4]Jerome Bruner, *On Knowing* (Cambridge: The Belknap Press of H. U. Press, 1962), pp. 82–83.

[5]Hilda Taba, *Teacher's Handbook for Elementary Social Studies* (Reading, Mass.: Addison-Wesley Publishing Company, Inc., 1967), p. 87.

objects in order to develop an intuitive grasp of the abstract concepts before he engages in abstract reasoning. Teaching strategies require the following of a proper developmental sequence.[6]

The teaching strategies which helped students advance to higher levels of thinking involved what questions were asked; what the teacher gave or sought and at which point in the proceedings; or bypassed elaboration and extension of ideas; and whether or not there were summaries of ideas and information before inferences of higher order were sought.[7]

As Taba so aptly points out, teaching children thinking skills depends more on what we get out of the children than on what we put in them.[8]

The basic philosophy of the problem-solving approach is one of developing in children thinking skills that enable them to formulate generalizations about a given situation. These generalizations should be ones that can be applied in new situations, specifically in the problems of the children's everyday lives.

Obviously, the conditions of learning within the classroom and the role of the teacher are crucial aspects of the problem-solving approach.

CLASSROOM CONDITIONS

The atmosphere of the classroom must foster within the children a feeling of trust and security. Students need to know that they will receive help and understanding from the teacher and that they can ask questions and offer acceptable answers without fear of being wrong. The classroom environment should provide excitement and stimulation for learning. Materials should be available to supply the needs of searching minds. The teacher should create an atmosphere of mental freedom that enables each individual to think without concern for boundaries.

ROLE OF THE TEACHER

In an inquiry-oriented classroom, the concept of the teacher's role undergoes a change in emphasis. Previously, the teacher assumed the major roles of information giver and disciplinarian with minor roles of motivator, referrer, counselor, and advisor.

In an inquiry-centered classroom, however, the teacher assumes the primary role of motivator while remaining an information giver, disciplinarian, counselor, referrer, and advisor.

[6]Taba, *Teacher's Handbook for Elementary Social Studies*, p. 88.
[7]Taba, *Teacher's Handbook for Elementary Social Studies*, p. 88.
[8]Taba, *Teacher's Handbook for Elementary Social Studies*, p. 89.

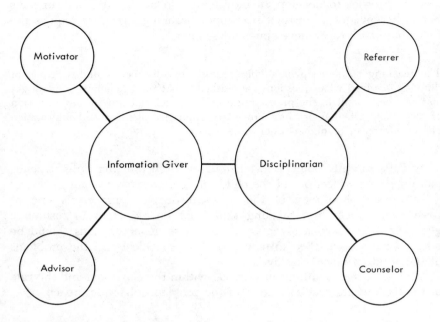

FIGURE 2. Previously, the teacher's major role was that of information giver and disciplinarian with minor roles of motivator, referrer, counselor, and advisor.

As motivator, the teacher stimulates and challenges his students to think. He initiates problem situations for the children to identify. His questioning provides the focus and direction for the children's search. He assumes the role of information giver only when his students request it or when it becomes necessary to redirect activities that may have wandered from the original goal. As referrer, he guides children to materials and sources of information. As advisor and counselor, he supplies children with encouragement when it is needed and he diagnoses difficulties and gives assistance. Discipline is necessary to avoid chaos; however, it is vital that children be guided toward self-discipline, which is important in the problem-solving approach.

Objectives

The objectives of the method of problem solving through inquiry are based on the processes or steps in which children are involved (identifying a problem, stating and testing hypotheses, and generalizing).

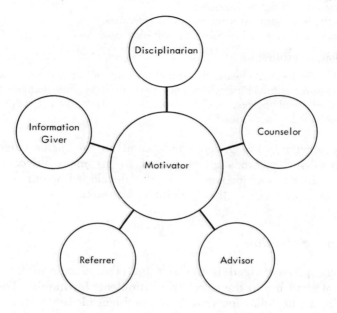

FIGURE 3. The teacher's major role in an inquiry-centered classroom is that of motivator with minor roles of information giver, disciplinarian, counselor, referrer, and advisor.

These broad objectives are outlined as follows:

Develop the student's ability:

To identify and define a problem situation in relation to the social sciences and to apply this knowledge to everyday life.

To formulate hypotheses for tentative problem solutions utilizing the information presented and previously acquired knowledge.

To compare and evaluate various theories, data, and generalizations in testing tentative hypotheses.

To select relevant facts necessary for testing hypotheses.

To state generalizations from results and apply them to new situations.

Acquire skill:

In the use of a variety of materials to secure information relative to the problem.

In discovering the relationships between previously and newly acquired information to acquire new insight into the solution of a problem.

In rational thought processes by constructing hypotheses and testing, revising, and refining these hypotheses.

In expressing opinions on issues after an analysis of available information.

Acquire knowledge:

Of problem-solving techniques.
Of methods of inquiry used by social scientists.
Of recall information necessary for problem solution.

Develop an attitude:

Of open-mindedness toward all sides of an issue before arriving at a decision.
Of accepting opinions of others and understanding why opinions vary.
Of concern and interest in the problems of society by active participation in problem-solving activities.[9]

These objectives are general and based on the major values of the problem-solving methods as purported by its many advocates. More specific behavioral objectives should be developed within the content boundaries and needs of the individual classroom.

Problem Selection

Quickly acknowledged is the fact that the success of the problem-solving method lies in the selection of problems for inquiry. Dunfee and Sagl suggest the following criteria for problem identification:

1. Does the problem challenge the children intellectually, stimulate critical thinking, allow them to seek cause-and-effect relationships, and offer opportunity for formulating and testing generalizations?
2. Does the problem relate directly to the lives of the children, based on their past experiences, and have an impact upon them presently?
3. Is the problem concerned with a basic human activity and does it thus illumine man's efforts to meet his needs?
4. Are there sufficient community and classroom instructional resources available for developing the problem?
5. Does the problem offer opportunities for expansion of interests?[10]

Does following the guidelines of a structured plan restrict the problem-solving method? Should teachers be permitted to provide alternatives to the suggested outline of study? Freedom of choice in what Clements, Fielder, and Tabachnick call "Big Questions" for inquiry study is "justified by the demands of a particular teaching-learning situation and its

[9]The writer acknowledges the use of Benjamin Bloom and David Krathwohl, *Taxonomy of Educational Objectives: Handbook I. The Cognitive Domain* (New York: David McKay Co., Inc., 1956).
[10]Maxine Dunfee and Helen Sagl, *Social Studies Through Problem Solving* (New York: Holt, Rinehart & Winston, Inc., 1966), pp. 23–24.

potential for increasing the efficiency with which children learn."[11] The choice of alternates for study should be based on:

1. Children's interests, questions, and attempts to interpret events.
2. Teacher's experiences and participation in community events and concerns.
3. Consideration of the work of various social scientists such as historian, geographer, or anthropologist.[12]

The "Big Questions" or problems should be interesting and should initiate inquiry. It should be possible to translate them into small questions that can be answered by simple observation and lead to increased understanding. By selecting concepts and ideas that help answer the small questions, answers to the "Big Questions" can be formulated.[13]

Fox, Lippitt, and Lohman, of the University of Michigan, assume "that the way for children to inquire in a social science area is to begin with incidents that are microcosms of the larger scene—incidents that are representative of their own life experiences."[14] An adaptation of their model of inquiry is presented:

1. Identify problem.
   Set goals.

   Make design for study.

   Why do people behave in this way?

2. Observation data collection.

   Children look for clues to determine why things turn out the way they do.

3. Advance theories for causes of behavior.

4. What behavior might lead to better consequences?

   Make hypothesis.

   Test hypothesis.

5. Draw conclusions.

6. Research theories of others.

7. Generalize.

   How can I apply this to my own life?[15]

[11]H. Millard Clements, William R. Fielder, and B. Robert Tabachnick, *Social Study: Inquiry in Elementary Classrooms* (Indianapolis: The Bobbs-Merrill Company, Inc., 1966), p. 117.

[12]Clements, Fielder, and Tabachnick, *Social Study: Inquiry in Elementary Classrooms*, pp. 118–21.

[13]Clements, Fielder, and Tabachnick, *Social Study: Inquiry in Elementary Classrooms*, p. 68.

[14]Robert Fox, Ronald Lippitt, and John Lohman, *Teaching of Social Science Material in the Elementary School*, USOE Cooperative Research Project E-011 (Ann Arbor, Michigan: University of Michigan, 1964), cited in Fair and Shaftel, eds., *Effective Thinking in the Social Studies*, p. 156.

[15]Fair and Shaftel, eds., *Effective Thinking in the Social Studies*, p. 157.

A sample program of the method of problem solving through inquiry will be developed with adaptations from the above model.

INITIATION

The initiation (designated in the model as Step 1) sets the stage for the problem-solving situation. It should stimulate inquiry and develop a continuing interest in the problem. Unless sufficient background is provided, problem identification will be difficult; however, too much information may stymie the quest. The initiation establishes the focus or direction of the search and serves as a springboard for action. The most effective initiations are those that actively involve the children, either mentally or physically. Possibilities for this stimulation are contained in these illustrations of initiations.

INCIDENT

This example from a sixth-grade classroom is designed to initiate inquiry. Step 1. The teacher, without giving any reason for his action, uses chairs and desks to build a separating wall between two sections of children in the classroom. He deliberately separates good friends and any brothers or sisters. The children soon ask questions. "Why are you doing this? What have we done to deserve this? My best friend is on the other side, when will we get to sit together again? How long are you going to leave this here?" As a result of this experience, the children begin to analyze the motives for and results of such actions. The remaining steps of the model are easily identified: Step 2. Observe the behavior of the children as the incident takes place. Help the children look for clues to help them understand their own behavior. Step 3. Advance theories about causes—what negative or positive feelings were produced? Step 4. What behavior might lead to better consequences? Was there some way to avoid the building of the wall? Make and test an hypothesis by classroom action. Step 5. Draw conclusions and summarize learnings. Step. 6. Discuss places in the world where cities or countries have been divided in such a manner—Berlin, Korea, Vietnam. By introducing questions and materials, the teacher can provide direction or focus toward one of these areas if he desires. The inquiry can now take on as much emphasis as necessary through research, reading, and discussion. Step 7. Generalizations can be drawn from the study. Final applications are made to the children's own life—a possible question might be "What behavior leads to hostile feelings toward me?"

PRESENTATION OF FACTS

Another activity designed to initiate inquiry is this graduated presentation of a series of facts about a country to a fifth-grade class.[16]

FIRST TRANSPARENCY

Comparison

Area: 142,726 sq. mi.	Area of California: 158,693 sq. mi.
Population: 98,865,955	Population of California: 15,717,204
Coastline: 16,654 mi.	Coastline of California: 3,427 mi.

Questions:

As you compare the area and population of this country with those of California, what conclusions can you draw?

What does the comparison of coastlines indicate?

From your limited knowledge of this country, identify any problems you think it might have.

Some problems the children might suggest would be overpopulation and lack of food.

SECOND TRANSPARENCY

Production (tons)

Coal	52,056,000	Gold
Pig Iron	20,436,000	Silver
Steel	31,500,000	Copper
Cement	29,952,000	Lead
Electricity	144,000 kwh	Zinc

Ships 2,389,000 tons under construction
Merchant fleet 15,000,000 tons

Questions:

Do these products give you any indication of the physical features of the country?

[16]Luman H. Long, ed., *The World Almanac* (New York: Newspaper Enterprise Association, Inc., 1968), pp. 325, 505.

What does the production of electricity indicate?

Does the number of tons of ships and merchant fleet indicate anything?

THIRD TRANSPARENCY

Agricultural Products

Tea	Pears	Cotton	Barley
Beans	Apples	Rice	Sweet and White Potatoes
Peaches	Grapes	Wheat	Tobacco

Questions:

What type of climate do these crops suggest?

Are there any discrepancies in the climate suggested by these crops?

Do the crops indicate the country's location?

FOURTH TRANSPARENCY

Imports (dollars)	Exports (dollars)
6,739,000,000	5,448,000,000
	(products)
	Clothing
	Metal Products
	Plywood
	Toys
	Chemical Fertilizers
	Ships
	Silk
	Optical Goods
	Automobiles

Questions:

What does the balance of exports and imports suggest about the economy of this country?

Do the products indicate any of the industries in the country?

Hypothesize concerning the problems you see facing this country.

Try to identify the country.

The country is Japan. The class can now begin to seek information to determine if Japan does face these problems. The information on the transparencies was selected to focus primarily on economics, but other facts can be selected to change focus.

ROLE-PLAYING

Role-playing is an activity that can be used for initiation in any grade. Following is an example of its use at the primary level. The teacher presents and discusses a particular situation with several selected children who, in turn, role-play for the class. Their dialogue follows:

KEVIN. Did you hear what happened to Billy on the playground yesterday?
SARAH. No, I was absent.
KEVIN. He was sliding backwards down the slide and cracked his head.
JESS. He's in the hospital with a concussion.
SARAH. I'm sorry, but he knows we shouldn't slide backwards.
KEVIN. He always did like to show off.
JESS. Other kids do it all the time and don't get hurt, so why shouldn't he?

Question:

Why do you suppose Billy behaved this way?

The class discusses the situation and recognizes the problems and consequences of breaking the safety rules. They try to understand why things turn out as they do. Why did Billy get hurt when others do the same thing without being hurt? What type of behavior would lead to better consequences? The class makes and tests hypotheses and draws conclusions. The teacher may then direct the search for information in any direction he prefers—for example, bike safety, home safety, or highway safety.

These examples of initiations are not intended to encompass all possibilities; they merely provide the teacher with a focal point.

CONTINUING ACTIVITIES

After the problem has been initiated to the class, the search for a solution may take many forms, dependent upon the needs of the class. For example, the class may be divided into committees (which will be discussed in chapter nine) to find and report to the class on answers to specific questions. Or individual research involving a variety of resource materials may prove more beneficial in a particular class situation.

Films or filmstrips presented to the whole class or to small groups may supply the needed information. Records or tapes may be used. Interviews of people within the school or community also help provide information. In this search for knowledge, the children often discover an association of facts and, thus, gain additional insight into the problem.

When sufficient knowledge or information has been acquired by the previously stated methods, the children can analyze their hypotheses in light of the newly acquired facts. They can then restate their hypotheses or draw generalizations based on their new knowledge. Applications of these generalizations to the children's own life should be attempted.

RESPONSIBILITY OF CHILDREN IN AN INQUIRY-CENTERED CLASSROOM

Active participation is required of the child at all times. Mental activity involving rational thought to identify problems and suggest possible solutions is a necessity for the child. He must be able to express his thoughts in a manner that can be understood by all. He must be open-minded and willing to accept the thoughts and opinions of others. He must not be fearful of making mistakes or overly concerned about whether his suggested answers or solutions are right or wrong.

Equally important in an inquiry-centered classroom is the child's ability to search for information from a number of sources. He must be able to look at all sides of an issue and make decisions in light of the information available to him. Insight into his own behavior is required to enable him to apply the generalizations to his own life.

Advantages and Disadvantages of Problem Solving Through Inquiry

Advocates of the method of problem solving through inquiry stress the value of developing rational thought and of the act of discovery encountered during the search for solutions to a problem. Bruner hypothesizes that discovery in learning "helps the child to learn the varieties of problem solving, of transforming knowledge for better use, helps him to learn how to go about the very task of learning."[17] Retrieval of the information learned through discovery is more easily accomplished.[18]

Motivation for learning becomes internal for the learner in the problem-solving situation, because he is actively seeking knowledge to solve a

[17]Bruner, *On Knowing*, p. 87.
[18]Bruner, *On Knowing*, p. 95.

given problem. The excitement of discovery encourages him to continue his search. He learns by doing.

The problems presented to the learner are concrete and are related directly to the child's own experiences. The child can suggest a variety of solutions. The situations remain open-ended and can lead to further study.

Those who question the inquiry method's emphasis on the act of discovery suggest that it places too little attention on the crucial role played by facts and skills in a student's mastery of a body of knowledge. Ausubel relates that "abundant experimental research has confirmed the proposition that prior learnings are not transferable to new learnings unless they are first overlearned."[19]

Friedlander questions the value of a child's curiosity in operating as a motivator and incentive for academic learning. He claims that children's curiosity may be unsystematic, noncumulative, immediate, and easily satisfied. He suggests that a child's curiosity may be satisfied with incorrect or partial information and that it may be strongest with issues not necessarily the proper concern of the school.[20]

Concern is voiced by many for the inquiry method's practice of accepting "any answer." This group stresses the fact that the child might not have the opportunity to test all of his answers and it questions how the child will know if his answers are right or wrong. Continued research is necessary to answer the claims of both the advocates and the opponents of this method.

SELECTED REFERENCES

Bruner, Jerome, *Toward A Theory of Instruction.* Cambridge: Harvard University Press, 1966.

Clements, H. Millard, William R. Fielder, and B. Robert Tabachnick, *Social Study: Inquiry in Elementary Classrooms.* Indianapolis: The Bobbs-Merrill Company, Inc., 1966.

Dunfee, Maxine and Helen Sagl, *Social Studies Through Problem Solving.* New York: Holt, Rinehart & Winston, Inc., 1966.

Fair, Jean and Fannie R. Shaftel, *Effective Thinking in the Social Studies.* Washington, D. C.: National Council for the Social Studies, 1967.

Fenton, Edwin, *Teaching the New Social Studies in Secondary Schools: An Inductive Approach.* New York: Holt, Rinehart & Winston, Inc., 1966.

[19]D. P. Ausubel, "A Teaching Strategy for Culturally Deprived Pupils: Cognitive and Motivational Considerations," *School Review,* LXXI (1963), 456.

[20]Bernard Z. Friedlander, "A Psychologist's Second Thoughts on Concepts, Curiosity, and Discovery in Learning," *Harvard Educational Review,* XXXV (1965), 25.

Goldmark, Bernice, *Social Studies, A Method of Inquiry*. Belmont, Calif.: Wadsworth Publishing Co., Inc., 1968.

Massialas, Byron G. and Benjamin C. Cox, *Inquiry in Social Studies*. New York: McGraw-Hill Book Company, Inc., 1966.

Schwab, Joseph J., *The Teaching of Science as Inquiry*. Cambridge: Harvard University Press, 1962.

Servey, Richard, *Social Studies Instruction in the Elementary School*. San Francisco: Chandler Publishing Co., 1967.

Suchman, J. Richard, *Developing Inquiry*. Chicago: Science Research Associates, 1966.

CHAPTER FOUR

Unit Development

CURRENT INTERPRETATIONS OF UNIT TEACHING ARE EQUAL IN variety and number to those of problem solving. The *Dictionary of Education* defines the unit as "an organization of learning activities, experiences, and types of learning around a central theme, problem, or purpose developed cooperatively by a group of pupils under teacher leadership."[1]

Michaelis identifies a unit as "a plan to achieve specific objectives through the use of content and learning activities related to a designated topic."[2] Another definition suggests "The unit represents a way of organizing materials and activities for instructional purposes."[3] Each definition recog-

[1]Carter V. Good, *Dictionary of Education* (New York: McGraw-Hill Book Company, Inc., 1945), p. 436.
[2]John U. Michaelis, *Social Studies in a Democracy* (Englewood Cliffs, N.J.: Prentice-Hall, Inc., 1968), p. 199.
[3]John Jarolimek, *Social Studies in Elementary Education* (New York: The Macmillan Company, 1967), p. 56.

55

nizes the importance of organizing learning activities. This organization is the key to unit planning—one learning experience must be related to another in order to avoid fragmentation. A unit contains learning experiences that are related to other curriculum areas—for example, language arts, math, science, physical education, art, and music. Problem solving may be incorporated in the unit, but a unit can be developed without its use.

Basically, there are two types of units—the resource unit and the teaching unit. Resource units, as the label indicates, contain extensive suggestions of learning experiences, content, and materials for developing a selected topic with children. In contrast, a teaching unit is created to meet the needs and interests of a specific group of children. The teacher may draw upon the contents of a resource unit for the development of a teaching unit. A teaching unit may become a resource unit when used by another teacher with a different group of children.

The organization of a unit consists of: (1) purpose—the reason for teaching the unit; (2) objectives—the goals that will be reached in the process of teaching the unit; (3) content—primarily the background information for the teacher or an organization of the knowledge necessary to achieve an understanding of the topic; (4) activities—including initiation, individual and group experiences, integration with other subject areas, and culmination; (5) bibliography—references for the teacher and children and materials such as records, films, filmstrips, and games; (6) evaluation—a measure of the success achieved in accomplishing established objectives. Variations occur in this suggested organization, but most units contain the same components.

Objectives

Objectives established for the unit method of teaching overlap with those of problem solving, because both methods are concerned with similar goals although they attempt to achieve their goals by different means. Broad objectives for unit teaching include:

Acquire skill:

In working cooperatively with members of a group through committee participation.

In the use of a variety of materials including books, primary sources, magazines, and pamphlets.

In communicating with members of a group through reports, plays, panel discussions, and interviews.

Develop an understanding:

Of the importance of establishing effective human relationships to achieve established goals.

Of the interrelationship of content areas.

Of the importance of social studies in relation to everyday life.

Of the democratic process and the responsibility of each individual to make the process effective.

Acquire knowledge:

Of facts and information sufficient to develop an understanding of the topic under study.

Of methods to secure accurate information about the topic.

Obviously, these objectives are quite general and are based on the elements of unit teaching that are emphasized. More specific behavioral objectives could be formulated with a definite topic in mind.

Unit teaching is based on the theory that the child is motivated to learn material that he helps select and plan in cooperation with his teacher. The theory also suggests that a child can understand a topic more readily if he studies it in the context of various subject areas, for he is then able to realize the interconnectedness of the content areas. Following this method, a child who is attempting to understand Russian culture, for example, learns about the country's music and art and participates in games played by Russian children in addition to learning about Russia's government, education, history, geography, and economics.

The unit is a blueprint for broad or depth coverage of a topic. Topics can be covered in breadth, including as many aspects as possible, or in depth, emphasizing only selected aspects. A unit generally requires a longer period of time than does a problem-solving situation. However, a problem-solving situation may be included as part of a unit. The unit method places more emphasis on content acquired than does the method of problem solving, but content is not its primary goal. The processes the child uses (communicating, cooperating, researching, and analyzing) as he acquires his information are still the primary goal. The fact that a unit-teaching situation provides opportunities to meet individual differences is one of its vital facets.

ROLE OF THE TEACHER

The teacher's role in unit teaching is similar to that in an inquiry-centered classroom, but there are some differences. The teacher's major role is still one of motivator; however, more of the initial motivation should come from the child's involvement in the planning. Because the teacher has developed the unit plan, he supplies more guidance for the organization of the study. There is cooperative teacher-pupil planning of learning experiences to permit children to participate in democratic processes. The teacher plans activities particularly designed to meet individual needs. The referrer role is expanded, for more information is provided directly by the teacher, who supplies materials for research and suggests activities for reporting. The child is involved in some discovery in pursuit of information, but it is not as greatly emphasized in unit teaching. Advisor and counselor roles remain the same, and discipline is provided through democratic procedures.

ROLE OF THE CHILDREN

Children's responsibilities during the development of a unit are extensive. They should actively participate in the planning stage of the unit, fulfill their committee obligations, enter into discussions, and report research findings to others. In addition, they should exhibit interest in the other children's reports, ask questions when necessary, and evaluate the performance of themselves and others.

Democratic procedures are formulated by the children, and it is each individual's responsibility to abide by the rules established. Group cooperation is necessary to accomplish the selected goals.

CONDITIONS OF THE CLASSROOM

The atmosphere of the classroom is created by the group's decisions concerning the regulation of their activities. Through cooperative planning, the children and teacher develop suggested behavior standards for working in committees, doing research, and presenting information to the class. The teacher's primary responsibility is to guide the children's thinking toward reasonable decisions. Extensive materials are necessary for research, and physical conditions should lend themselves to small group activities.

Unit Selection

Numerous criteria are suggested for selecting units of study around children's interests. Some of these criteria are: (1) the unit's general utility, (2) its social significance, (3) its ability to increase and extend the children's background knowledge, and (4) consideration of the needs and demands of society.[4] If the processes in which children are involved (communicating, cooperating, researching, and analyzing) constitute the primary goal of unit development, should the content of the unit be based on the interests of children? Will children become more involved in a unit based on their interests? What are the interests of children at the various grade levels? Research indicates that children are interested in:

First grade—Trips or journeys to extraordinary and different places such as dry, wet, hot, or cold lands. Also, cowboys and Indians of early American history.

Second grade—Areas of the earth different from their own immediate environment such as Africa, Japan, the North Pole. Historical background of national symbols as Fourth of July, Statue of Liberty, the President.

Third grade—Big oceans and big continents, historical background of people such as Indians, soldiers of the Revolution, the person who discovered New York.

Fourth grade—Genuine interests in particular areas of the earth—Japan, England, the Congo and general social features of these such as the Queen of England, the religion of Japan.

Fifth grade—Those geographic areas which dominate the current news—Middle East, Russia, China and the historical reason for some of the large social problems that appear on the national and international scene.

Sixth grade—Similar interests as the fifth grade, but more penetrating. Also, interest in the poverty of the masses in Latin America, social differences in East and West, beginnings of Communism, and development of the Cold War.[5]

Do the children's interests change as the times change? Are their interests universal, or do they differ from school to school and from classroom to classroom? How can the teacher determine the interests of the children in his classroom?

The teacher can develop an interest inventory to aid in determining the focus of his students' interests. The children answer the teacher's questions by checking the appropriate column, for example, "like," "dislike," or "not sure." Sample questions might be:

1. Do you like to learn about the following?
   a. People from countries such as
      Japan?
      Vietnam?
      Africa?

[4]Jarolimek, *Social Studies in Elementary Education*, pp. 44–45.
[5]William Ragan and John D. McAulay, *Social Studies for Today's Children* (New York: Appleton-Century-Crofts, Inc., 1964), pp. 201–2.

   b. The way a country runs its government?
   c. Why many people in the world cannot find work and do not have enough food to eat?
   d. Famous people such as
      John F. Kennedy?
      Queen Elizabeth?
      Charles De Gaulle?
   e. How people transport goods from place to place by
      Trains?
      Airplanes?
      Ships?

Teachers formulate questions based on current topics in the news, suggested topics from curriculum guides, and knowledge of the children's interests gleaned from class and informal discussions. Other types of interest inventories might involve short answer questions, children's autobiographies, or individual pupil-teacher conferences.

Directing Children's Interests

Children's interests can be directed toward topics that the teacher deems important for study. The techniques that the teacher employs to introduce the topic as well as the interest displayed by him are important factors. What topics should be included in the elementary-school social studies? The basic human activities involved in the expanding communities of men (in the family, school, neighborhood, local county and metropolitan area, state, region of states, U.S. national, U.S. and inter-American, U.S. and Atlantic, U.S. and Pacific, and in the World), as identified by Hanna, are frequently used as a basis for determining content. These activities are:

1. Producing, exchanging, distributing, and consuming food, clothing, shelter, and other consumer goods and services.
2. Communicating ideas and feelings.
3. Organizing and governing.
4. Transporting people and goods.
5. Protecting and conserving human and natural resources.
6. Creating tools, technics, and social arrangements.

7. Providing recreation.
8. Expressing religious impulses.
9. Expressing and satisfying aesthetic impulses.
10. Providing education.[6]

Equally important to consider for inclusion in a social studies unit are topics that aid in developing the selected generalizations from each of the social sciences: history, geography, sociology, economics, political science, anthropology, philosophy, and psychology.[7]

An awareness of our current social, economic, and political problems should certainly direct the teacher's selection of topics. The ever important aspect of perpetuating our democratic heritage should also be considered.

Development of a Unit

INITIATION

The teacher is responsible for providing the setting for the study. Sufficient information is necessary to stimulate continuing interest in a topic. A problem-solving situation, as suggested in chapter three, can be used for the introduction in order to combine the methods of problem solving and unit organization. Other initiation activities might include an arranged environment, exploratory questioning, films, stories, poetry, or folk tales.

ARRANGED ENVIRONMENT

Use of a number of prepared exhibits and bulletin boards creates a classroom atmosphere that lends itself to the topic for study. Bulletin boards supply two types of stimulation—(1) information about the topic, presented by charts, pictures, and newspaper clippings or (2) the presentation of a series of searching questions to be answered during the study.

Displays might include books and magazines that present discussions

---

[6]Paul R. Hanna, "Revising the Social Studies: What is Needed?," *Social Education*, XXVII (April, 1963), 190–96.

[7]*Social Studies Framework for the Public Schools of California* (Sacramento, Calif.: California State Department of Education, 1962), pp. 90–109.

of the topic at varying levels of reading difficulty. The books might contain stories as well as facts. Other displays might show selected artifacts relative to the topic.

Criticism of the arranged environment points out that it lacks pupil-teacher planning and sets an artificial beginning for the pursuit of the study. Gradual development of the bulletin boards and exhibits by the children throughout the study is suggested.

EXPLORATORY QUESTIONING

Teachers need to know the extent of their students' understanding or misunderstanding about a topic prior to beginning the study. Introducing a topic through a stimulating question period provides the teacher with information to help him plan the direction and depth of the study. It also creates excitement about the topic. Such questioning can be incorporated with any initiation or used exclusively for the initiation. For example, when the topic is concerned with Communism and the Russian way of life, the teacher might have the children react to questions such as: (1) What does Communism mean to you? (2) What would your life be like living under a Communistic government? (3) What are some of the contributions the Russians have made to our heritage?

Generally, more information about individual understanding can be obtained when children are requested to write their answers; however, oral questioning stimulates more interest in the topic. Assessment of the answers in terms of general misconceptions as well as the amount of present knowledge about the topic should direct the focus of the study.

FILM OR FILMSTRIP PRESENTATION

A film or filmstrip used to introduce the study can present information and/or questions. The presentation of too much information stifles interest in the topic. For example, a lengthy film covering most aspects of the Russian way of life would be used unwisely as an initiation.

READING STORIES, POETRY, OR FOLK TALES

Stories relative to the topic that present situations similar to those in the children's lives provide stimulation. Poetry and folk tales also catch the interest of the children. *Children's Books to Enrich the Social Studies* is a good source for information concerning this type of material.[8]

[8]Helen Huus, *Children's Books to Enrich the Social Studies* (Washington, D.C.: National Council for the Social Studies, 1966).

Teacher-Pupil Planning for the Unit

After the initiation has been completed, the course of action for the study should be planned cooperatively by the pupils and the teacher. The initiation in this example introduces Communism to a group of sixth graders with an excerpt from *Your World and Mine*. This story describes a conversation between a brother and sister concerning the problems they face going to work in a Russian factory away from their families.

"What is the trouble, Alexei? Didn't your lessons go well today?"

The brother and sister walked in silence for a minute. The snow squeaked beneath their heavy shoes, and it was growing dark. A crowded trolley car rattled by. Then a voice came from Alexei's muffler.

"No. I didn't finish the problems."

"I'm sorry," said Karla. "Was the teacher cross?"

"No," said Alexei again. "But she looked at me as if she thought I was dumb. I know I'm not stupid, Karla, am I?"

"Of course you're not," replied his sister. "It's because of working at the shoeshop all morning. I get tired, too. Your mind isn't so quick when you're tired. It was better, wasn't it, when your class had lessons in the morning and you worked in the shop in the afternoon?"

"Yes," agreed the boy, "it was better. But anyway I am not so good at lessons in this school as I was at home."

Karla made no reply to this. She knew that Alexei was homesick for the little farming village. He had liked their village school. He did not like the trade school he was going to now. But at least he had not had to come alone.

Karla was only fifteen, but she felt much older than fourteen-year-old Alexei. She felt sorry for her brother. She herself did not miss the village life so much.

"I wish we could go back to the farm and be with Mother, Father, and Petrya," Alexei was saying. "But even there we have to do what the Committee says." He sighed. "It would be nice to do what we wanted sometimes instead of always being told what to do by the Committee."

Karla glanced about anxiously.

"Don't say that, Alexei," she told him. "Remember what happens when you say anything against the government. We are lucky to be able to share a room with Aunt Sophie. The others who came from our village have had to live in that big building near the factory. You know you wouldn't like living there, would you, now?"

"No, I shouldn't," admitted the boy. "But I do hope we can go back to the country this summer."

"Probably we shall," said Karla. "They usually need young people from the city to help harvest. But here we are at the store."

On the shelf behind the counter were long loaves of dark rye bread. The girl in the white jacket gave Karla a loaf, and Karla counted out the coins to pay for it. A little way beyond the grocery store they turned into the dooryard of a square cottage.

"Think how lucky we were to find this place to live," she reminded Alexei. "One big room for the three of us is a pretty fine home. So many people are living crowded in with other families. Besides, Aunt Sophie has been so good to us, it has made a lot of difference."

"You are right, Karla," said the boy. "We are lucky, and I did not mean to grumble. Let's get things ready for supper before Sophie gets home."

Inside they quickly pulled off their wraps. Karla spread a cloth over the table, and laid a knife beside the loaf. From a cupboard Alexei brought glasses for the tea, and three heavy bowls. There were steps in the hall outside, and Karla ran to open the door.

"Come in, Aunt Sophie," she cried. "We just got home. Are you tired?"

Aunt Sophie was tall. Bundled in her thick coat and head-shawl she looked very big. Alexei jumped to take her coat. Then, while she sat in one of the straight wooden chairs, he and Karla each tugged off one of her boots. They were heavy gray felt boots which came to her knees.

"Listen," said Sophie, "I have news. What do you think? I was top in my department at the factory today! Yes, after only six months, top! I finished more razor blades than any other worker! I will get a prize!"

Alexei sighed. "That will never happen to me. I'm just not able to work fast in a factory. I want to be a farmer."[9]

This is a dialogue that might follow this reading:

TEACHER. What is different about your life and that of these children in Russia?

SAM. They work in a factory while they are in school.

ALICE. They live away from their families.

JIM. The Committee tells them what to do. What is the Committee?

TEACHER. Does anyone know?

JEFF. It has something to do with Communism. They're like police.

FRAN. No, I think the Committee is just a group of the Russian people who are Communists.

TEACHER. Aren't all the people in Russia Communists?

SAM. I don't think so, but the Communists control the government and tell the people what to do.

TEACHER. Can people work wherever they prefer in Russia?

JEFF. No, they work together for the government.

TEACHER. Why?

JEFF. I don't know.

TEACHER. What information do we need to answer these questions?

ALICE. We need to know how the government works.

JEFF. I want to know how the people live. The story said houses were hard to find.

JIM. Why does Russia have Communism?

FRAN. What is the country like and what kind of crops grow there?

[9]Grace Dawson, *Your World and Mine* (Boston: Ginn & Company, 1965), pp. 273–74.

BILL. Aren't some other countries Communist?

TEACHER. We have several topics listed for research—How the Government Works, Why Russia is Communist, How the People Live, Geography, Crops, and Industry, and Other Communist Countries. Is there anything more you want to know about Russia?

JEFF. Aren't the Russians famous for their music and dancing?

TEACHER. Yes, let's add that to our list. Look carefully at the topics and decide which one you want to choose for research.

MARY. Can we work in committees, so several people can look for information on each topic?

TEACHER. Good idea. We should find more information when we work together on a problem.

Children become more actively involved in their learning experiences when they have an opportunity to share in the planning. The teacher can easily guide the discussion toward the goals he plans to accomplish.

Individual and Group Activities

Unit organization has the advantage of offering the opportunity to meet individual needs. Children who have special interests or skills can be guided toward tasks that fulfill these needs. Research can be conducted in areas of a study that are of particular interest to individual children. Those of exceptional ability can engage in research in greater depth and can thus acquire skills beyond the normal level. Children who have talent in music, art, writing, or drama have an opportunity to use these skills.

Group activities also contribute to the individual's development. For example, the child who has difficulty in getting along with other children who is assigned to a group activity of real interest to him will, hopefully, acquire skills of cooperative behavior. Equally important is the opportunity for the child with leadership ability to channel this energy into worthwhile activities. Shy children who would hesitate to enter into activities and discussions before the total group will often do so within small groups.

Group activities might include committee work in research or other projects. Other activities might involve participation in panel discussions or debates (discussed in chapter nine), which provide for cooperative planning and group interaction. Activities that encourage discussions of important aspects in the study aid the development of oral language skills.

Integrating Activities

The development of an understanding of the relationship of one subject area to another is made possible through integrating activities, which help children realize that knowledge in one subject is related to other subject areas. These activities also provide meaningful practice of skills acquired in other areas.

LANGUAGE ARTS

Skills introduced in the language arts acquire more meaning when they are applied in the content areas. Children realize a purpose for acquiring skills when they can put them to use. Unit teaching provides numerous opportunities for the use of language skills.

Methods for encouraging the development of oral language skills might include reports of individual or committee research, panel discussions or debates on facets of the study, role-playing incidents to clarify understandings, and class discussions about the topics. Interviewing individuals to secure information also develops oral language skills. Listening skills, too, are sharpened during these experiences.

Outlining, note taking, and preparing written reports are skills needed for research activities. Locational skills involving use of the table of contents, index, cross references, and appendix are necessary when seeking information during the study.

ART, MUSIC, AND PHYSICAL EDUCATION

Construction activities such as building a model Indian village or a salt and flour relief map add considerable understanding to a study and correlate learning experiences. Painting or drawing murals provides opportunity for interpreting events. Making artifacts from various cultures (for example, a teepee when studying Indians) makes a study more realistic.

Frequently, topics provide opportunity for integration with music (for example, constructing maracas or drums when studying Mexico or listening to the music of the country). Learning the dances native to a country helps develop an understanding of the people. Children enjoy learning the games that are played in the countries under study.

Culminating Activities

Culminating activities draw together the learning experiences of the unit. These activities should emphasize the main points, identify the inter-related ideas, and provide a composite view of the topic. As a result of these activities, children should be able to formulate generalizations that can be applied to new situations. Examples of culminating experiences follow:

COMMITTEE REPORTS

The completed research of the committees can be presented in a variety of ways—T.V. or radio productions; talks illustrated with prepared charts, bulletin boards, and realia; or a movie roll that includes information from every committee.

TOURS

The study of a country provides the opportunity for planning a guided tour to emphasize the important historic, recreational, and geographic points of interest. Illustrative materials such as maps, murals, and pictures supply background.

DRAMATIZATIONS

The production of dramatic presentations requires interpretation of the information secured and insures better understanding of the topic. Children portraying the landing of the Pilgrims or the Boston Tea Party will understand better and retain longer the information acquired.

FILMS AND FILMSTRIPS

Audiovisual aids such as films and filmstrips can be used effectively for culminating activities when they review information previously investigated.

Bibliography

An extensive bibliography listing the materials available for the teacher and the children should be included in the unit. Resource books, films, tapes, records, pictures, community resources, and suggested field trips should be included for reference.

Evaluation

The methods of evaluation to be utilized during and at the completion of the unit should be planned. The evaluation is an attempt to determine whether or not the objectives of the unit were successfully achieved. Evaluation must be made in terms of the success with which individual and group performance meets the objectives. Continuous evaluation throughout the unit guides its direction. The teacher should be evaluating his teaching procedures and his effectiveness in guiding the activities of the children. An assessment of the kind and use of materials is also important. Evaluation methods will be discussed in chapter twelve.

A Sample Resource Unit

Russia and Communism will be the topic used in this sample to illustrate the development of the aspects of a resource unit: purpose, generalizations, objectives, activities, and bibliography. The content or background information for the teacher is too extensive for inclusion here, but a skeletal outline is provided.

U.S.S.R.—RUSSIA—A LAND OF CONTRASTS

How Does Communism Affect the Lives of the Russian People?

Purpose: For many years the United States has been involved with Russia in a Cold War that results from differences in ideology concerning ownership of property and governmental control of people's activities. Children are confronted daily with references to Communism and Russia through newspapers, magazines, and television; however, they frequently do not have sufficient knowledge to understand these references. Because most of our country's international relationships and the future of the United States as a world leader are affected by current differences in ideology, it is vital that children acquire knowledge about Russia and Communism. Children should be able to compare and contrast Russia and Communism with the United States and Democracy to formulate their own opinions.

Initiation: A preliminary survey of the concepts or misconceptions children have about Communism should prove fruitful to guide the direction of the study. This unit of study will be formally initiated with the selection from *Your World and Mine* cited on pages 63–64. Follow-up discussion will pinpoint the children's concerns and questions.

GENERALIZATIONS	OBJECTIVES	CONTENT	LEARNING EXPERIENCES	RESOURCES

Geography influences the culture developed within a country and thus modifies the environment.	To acquire knowledge of the topography of Russia and to understand its effect on the country's cultural development.	I. Geography
		A. Area
		B. Population
		C. Location
		D. Land forms
		  1. Tundra
		  2. Taiga
		  3. Farming belt
		  4. Steppe
		  5. Desert
		  6. Mountains
		E. Rivers
			Discuss the location of Russia in relation to the United States and other areas of the world.	Filmstrip—*Geography of the Soviet Union* by Jam Handy

	To develop locational skills using maps and globes.		Organize a committee of children to make a model relief map of Russia from colored plasticene or flour and salt.	Relief maps and globes of the world.
	To develop skill in understanding and using the seven color key on a map or globe.	F. Natural resources G. Leading products	Take an imaginary trip through the geographic regions of Russia, pointing out the important features of each area.	Paul Hanna et al., *Beyond the Americas* (Chicago: Scott Foresman, 1964).

Culture is the pattern of interaction within a given group of people; it is determined by the people's shared values, beliefs, and opinions on acceptable behavior and customs.	To learn the cultural patterns of the people of Russia. To develop skill in locating information through a variety of sources.	H. People
		  1. Slavic
		  2. Turko-Tartar
		  3. Mongolian
			Organize committees to research topics such as Russian Life, Culture, Educational Systems, History, and Government.	R. W. Cordier, *History of World Peoples* (New York: Rand McNally & Co., 1949).

GENERALIZATIONS	OBJECTIVES	CONTENT	LEARNING EXPERIENCES	RESOURCES
	To develop the ability to work cooperatively through committee work.	I. Cities 1. Leningrad 2. Moscow 3. Stalingrad 4. Kiev 5. Vladivostok		Louis Snyder, *The First Book of the Soviet Union* (New York: Franklin Watts, Inc., 1959).
The educational system of a country perpetuates the culture of that country.	To develop oral language skills by reporting information to the class.	J. Agriculture-collective farms K. Education L. Recreation M. Music N. Art O. Religion		Thomas T. Hammond, "An American in Mockba: Russia's Capital," *National Geographic Magazine*, CXXIX, No. 3 (March, 1966), 297–351.
The historical background of a country affects its development.	To learn about the historical background of Russia in order to understand the country's present condition.	II. Historical events A. 200–300 A.D. Early peoples B. 900–First dynasty C. 1237– Mongolian invasion	Prepare a time line of the historical events in Russia. Have committees present reports through dramatizations, panel discussions, murals, graphs, and charts.	Dean Conger, "Siberia: Russia's Frozen Frontier," *National Geographic Magazine*, CXXXI, No. 3 (March, 1967), 297–347.

To learn how Communism controls Russia's government and to compare Russia's government with that of the United States.

To develop the ability to read critically and understand the writer's viewpoint.

Government is an attempt to give order and stability to a society.

D. 1547–1584 Ivan the Terrible
E. 1682–1725 Peter the Great
F. 1812 Napoleon's invasion
G. 1867 Alaska sold
H. 1917 Bolshevik Revolution
I. 1927 Lenin's death
J. 1928 Stalin
K. 1941 German invasion
L. 1953 Stalin's death
M. 1953–1968 Series of leaders

Listen to selections of Russian music, learn folk dances, and view filmstrips of physical education classes.

Film
The Soviet Union: An Introduction by Grover-Jennings Production, Monterey, California.

Kathleen Taylor, *The Lands and Peoples of the U.S.S.R.* (New York: The Macmillan Company, 1961).

71

GENERALIZATIONS	OBJECTIVES	CONTENT	LEARNING EXPERIENCES	RESOURCES
To be effective, a government must have the support of its people.	To be openminded enough to view both sides of an issue and formulate one's own opinion.	III. Government-Communist Dictatorship A. Divisions of government B. How Communism rules 1. Industry 2. Agriculture 3. Newspapers 4. Police state 5. Propaganda	Prepare a chart based on the comparison of the governmental divisions of Russia and the United States. Develop debate on the question: Are there personal freedoms in Russia?	Michael Shapovalou, *Let's Read About Russia* (Grand Rapids: Fideler Company, 1950).

72

Culminating Activities: Develop a mock meeting of the Security Council of the United Nations in which the United States and Russia debate an issue of current concern that requires knowledge of the beliefs and aspirations of both countries. Also, show a series of filmstrips of various aspects of Russia to review the lesson.

Advantages and Disadvantages of Unit Teaching

Most proponents of unit teaching claim that its major advantage is its broad or depth coverage of a topic, which provides opportunities for integration with other curriculum areas.

A unit also aids efficient organization of learning experiences. The boundaries of content for a topic are established to determine the skills, knowledge, attitudes, and understanding a child will acquire in a set period of time.[10]

The variety of activities possible in a unit provides opportunities for meeting individual needs. Also, this variation allows for the development of a wider range of skills.

The disadvantages of unit teaching are centered primarily on its inability to develop children's thinking skills. Problem solving through inquiry, which can be part of a unit, accomplishes this goal to a greater extent. The boundary lines drawn for the unit's content do not permit children to pursue interests that may arise spontaneously.

Possibly the most effective way of overcoming the disadvantages of both unit teaching and problem solving is to combine both methods. Hanna relates "that when the problem approach is used as the basis for unit organization the overall problem is analyzed into subproblems, and questions, the answers to which are necessary before the overall problem can be solved. Sometimes the larger problem grows out of a perplexity about a smaller, related problem."[11]

Obviously some topics that should be presented by unit organization don't lend themselves to problem solving or present such weak problem situations that they are ineffective. There are also some problem situations that can't be effectively organized as a unit because of their short-term duration. The teacher must select the most effective method by considering a topic in relation to the interest, ability, and motivation of his children.

[10]Ragan and McAulay, *Social Studies for Today's Children*, p. 217.
[11]Lavone A. Hanna, Gladys Potter, and Neva Hageman, *Unit Teaching in the Elementary School* (New York: Holt, Rinehart & Winston, Inc., 1963), pp. 233–34.

SELECTED REFERENCES

Darrow, Helen Fisher, *Social Studies for Understanding.* New York: Teachers College, Columbia University, 1964.

Hanna, Lavone A., Gladys Potter, and Neva Hageman, *Unit Teaching in the Elementary School.* New York: Holt, Rinehart & Winston, Inc., 1963.

Hill, Wilhelmina, *Unit Planning and Teaching in Elementary Social Studies.* Washington, D.C.: U.S. Office of Education, 1963.

Jarolimek, John, *Social Studies in Elementary Education* (3rd ed.). New York: The Macmillan Company, 1967.

Joyce, Bruce R., *Strategies for Elementary Social Science Education.* Chicago: Science Research Associates, Inc., 1965.

Michaelis, John U., *Social Studies for Children in a Democracy.* Englewood Cliffs, N.J.: Prentice-Hall, Inc., 1968.

Michaelis, John U., ed., *Teaching Units in the Social Sciences: Early Grades, Middle Grades, Intermediate Grades.* Chicago: Rand McNally & Co., 1966.

Ragan, William and John D. McAulay, *Social Studies for Today's Children.* New York: Appleton-Century-Crofts, Inc., 1964.

CHAPTER FIVE

Structure as a Method of Teaching

MUCH DISCUSSION CENTERS AROUND THE STRUCTURE OF THE social science disciplines. The discussion involves an identification of the structure of the disciplines and the role of structure in teaching. It also involves a determination of what learning experiences allow children to acquire knowledge of a discipline's structure. Before we define structure, it will be beneficial to discuss the meaning of "a discipline." A discipline is a body of knowledge about a subject, the individuals who investigate the subject, the methods of inquiry used by the discipline, and the desired outcomes of the inquiry. It is difficult to determine the membership and organization of the social science disciplines—to identify the disciplines that are significantly different—for they are all concerned with the study of human behavior. In the social sciences, the disciplines have been identified as history, geography, economics, political science, anthropology, **sociology**, psychology, and philosophy. After a discipline has been identified, its structure is sought.

Bruner relates "To learn structure, in short, is to learn how things are related."[1] He claims, "in order for a person to be able to recognize the applicability or inapplicability of an idea to a new situation and to broaden his learning thereby, he must have clearly in mind the general nature of the phenomenon with which he is dealing."[2] In other words, the individual must know the structure of the subject. However, to know how things are related without developing "an attitude toward learning and inquiry, toward guessing and hunches, toward the possibility of solving problems on one's own"[3] is learning that is not usable and meaningful. Joyce explains structure as organizing concepts, which formulate the way we think things are related.[4] These organizing concepts "provide the child with a systematic method of attack on areas where he seeks new knowledge."[5] The difficult task of the social scientist is to "translate the scholarly concepts and methods into forms that can be readily taught to children."[6] When these scholarly concepts have been selected and translated, experiences that permit children to discover their structure or organizing concepts should be selected.

Schwab states that the structure of a discipline is based on two components—concepts and syntax. "The conceptual structure of a discipline determines what we shall seek the truth about and in what terms the truth shall be couched. The syntactical structure of a discipline is concerned with the operations that distinguish the true, the verified, and the warranted in that discipline from the unverified and unwarranted. Both of these—the conceptual and syntactical—are different in different disciplines."[7]

Should concepts be presented in a sequence to provide an understanding of the discipline? Concept is defined as a "logical or analytical structure which groups objects or phenomena within one class or category."[8] Should all concepts be introduced at the beginning level and allowed to gain depth at each succeeding grade level, or should a set of concepts be presented at each level? The following diagrams will help clarify this understanding.

[1] Jerome S. Bruner, *The Process of Education* (Cambridge: Harvard University Press, 1960), p. 7.

[2] Bruner, *The Process of Education*, p. 18.

[3] Bruner, *The Process of Education*, p. 20.

[4] Bruce R. Joyce, *Strategies for Elementary Social Science Education* (Chicago: Science Research Associates, Inc.), p. 25.   © 1971 by Science Research Associates. Reprinted by permission.

[5] Joyce, *Strategies for Elementary Social Science Education*, p. 29.

[6] Joyce, *Strategies for Elementary Social Science Education*, p. 37.

[7] Joseph J. Schwab, "The Concept of the Structure of a Discipline," *Educational Record*, XLIII (July, 1962), 197–205.

[8] Byron G. Massialas and C. Benjamin Cox, *Inquiry in Social Studies* (New York: McGraw-Hill Book Company, Inc., 1966), p. 47.

Figure 4 illustrates the method of introducing a concept at the beginning level and allowing it to increase in depth at each succeeding level.

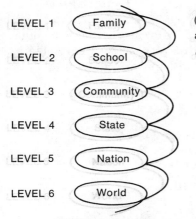

LEVEL 1 — Family

LEVEL 2 — School

LEVEL 3 — Community

LEVEL 4 — State

LEVEL 5 — Nation

LEVEL 6 — World

(Political science, sociology, economics, anthropology, history, geography, psychology, and philosophy.)

FIGURE 4. Concept of man organizing systems to reach certain goals.

LEVEL 1

Concept of interdependence of man (family, school, community, other people).

Concept of man's interaction with his environment (clothing, food, shelter).

LEVEL 2

Concept of man satisfying his needs with available resources (money, work, division of labor).

Concept of producing goods and services.

FIGURE 5. Selected set of concepts to be presented at each level.

In both examples, concepts are presented within a structure that is dependent (1) on the depth of the concept and (2) on one's previous set of concepts.

Social studies compounds the difficulty of introducing its structural framework, because it draws its content from a number of disciplines. Should the approach be interdisciplinary or multidisciplinary?

Advocates of the interdisciplinary approach view "the social sciences as specializations of a common subject matter. According to this view, one thinks of social science as a substantial subject that proliferates like the branches of a tree."[9]

Advocates of the multidisciplinary position see "the social sciences as independent sciences concerned with aspects of human behavior which are related by the fact that the behavior is performed by the same organism. Here the social sciences are not part of a single tree, but are a number of independently rooted trees that happen to grow in the same earth, the study of human behavior."[10]

FIGURE 6. Representation of the interdisciplinary approach. Each of the disciplines is related to the others through the common core of human behavior.

Those favoring the interdisciplinary approach stress the need to understand the interrelationships of the concepts of each of the social sciences. Presno and Presno explain that social science disciplines have some "common elements whatever their unique qualities and differences."[11] Each discipline "addresses itself to the description, explanation, and classification of some aspect of the goal-directed behavior of human

[9]G. W. Ford and Lawrence Pugno, eds., *The Structure of Knowledge and the Curriculum* (Chicago: Rand McNally & Co., 1964), p. 89.

[10]Ford and Pugno, eds., *The Structure of Knowledge and the Curriculum*, p. 89.

[11]Vincent Presno and Carol Presno, *Man in Action Series: People and Their Actions*, Teachers' Ed. (Englewood Cliffs, N.J.: Prentice-Hall, Inc., 1967), p. ix.

beings as they act, either individually or in groups, and as they are influenced by natural and cultural forces."[12]

Opponents of this theory argue that each discipline should retain its unique method of inquiry and conceptual structure. Scriven questions the interdisciplinary approach. He states that "the minute that you merge them, you get a smudge from which very little emerges."[13] Joyce, however, assumes "that the social sciences have much content in common and that a curriculum can be organized which emphasizes the unique concepts of each of them but does not establish separate courses for them."[14]

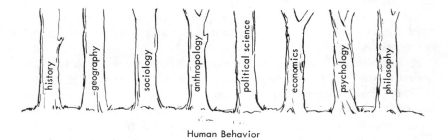

Human Behavior

FIGURE 7. Representation of the multidisciplinary approach.

The multidisciplinary approach might be further identified as a separate-subject approach; however, acquiring knowledge of the discipline without the method of inquiry is not its intent. Programs using both models have been developed. Examples of each will be discussed.

Philosophy of the Approach

Differences of opinion arise concerning whether the structure of a discipline actually provides a method for teaching the discipline. Certainly, the concepts of a discipline can be presented by the unit or problem-solving method; however, if they are not introduced in sequen-

[12]Presno, *Man in Action Series*, p. ix.
[13]Ford and Pugno, eds., *The Structure of Knowledge and the Curriculum*, p. 95.
[14]Joyce, *Strategies for Elementary Social Science Education*, p. 13.   © 1971 by Science Research Associates. Reprinted by permission.

tial order, it is doubtful that the structure of the discipline will be discovered. Teachers often have difficulty arranging an effective sequence
of activities for programs based on concepts. A study was recently conducted with beginning teachers to determine their ability in organizing
a sequence of learning activities for a concept-based social studies program. Findings revealed "that the chief difficulty encountered had to
do with selecting and providing relevant learning experiences for pupils.
Relating specific learning activities to the attainment of specific concepts
and generalizations proved to be particularly bothersome."[15] The pre-
vailing trend in prepared programs based on the disciplines is to provide
a sequential development of the concepts constituting a method.

The philosophy underlying the use of structure as a method of teaching
social studies is that the structure dictates what concepts will be presented and when. The prepared programs also suggest activities to be
used for teaching the concepts, although variations in these activities
are possible.

Programs based on structural framework have tight content boundary
lines to avoid confusing the children with other concepts presented at
the same time. A logical sequential program is planned, with each activity
leading to the development of the intended concept. Each activity in the
series builds upon the foundation provided by the previous activity.
These programs suggest the procedures to be used to achieve the best
results. As indicated previously, the structural framework is used to develop an understanding of the disciplines: the content, method of inquiry,
and goals.

ROLE OF THE TEACHER

The teacher needs a substantial background in the content of the
disciplines to adequately prepare him for his role as motivator and guide.
He must understand the concepts of the disciplines to be able to guide
the discussions and use the correct vocabulary. Because many elementary
teachers do not have sufficient foundations in the social science disciplines,
most programs provide extensive background guides for teachers.

It is vital that the teacher be enthusiastic about the programs in order
to prevent them from becoming a series of didactic lessons. A program's
suggested enrichment and extension activities (which use visual aids,
construction, children's books, and poetry to strengthen the concepts) are
an important part of the program. The classroom conditions suggested for

---

[15]Agnes M. Inn, "Beginning Teacher's Problems in Developing Social Studies
Concepts," *Social Education*, November, 1966, p. 540.

programs based on a structural framework are the same as those previously suggested for the other teaching methods.

Multidisciplinary Program

The following program, selected to present an example of a multidisciplinary approach, was developed by the Northwest Council for Economic Education under the supervision of the Office of the State Superintendent of Public Instruction, Olympia, Washington. This program provides for the development of a selected number of economic concepts at each grade level. The concepts for kindergarten through grade 6 follow:

CONCEPT SUMMARY

Kindergarten

Economic Concept I
   People are interdependent.
Economic Concept II
   All people are confronted with the conflict between unlimited wants and limited resources.
Economic Concept III
   Human wants are satisfied by goods that are either free goods or economic goods.
Economic Concept IV
   Income is earned by producing goods and services.

Grade one

Economic Concept I
   The basic economic problem confronting all people is the conflict between unlimited wants and limited resources.
Economic Concept II
   Goods and services are created by the production process. Individuals who contribute to the process receive a share of the goods and services.
Economic Concept III
   The development of specialization has made people more interdependent.
Economic Concept IV
   In our private enterprise economy, individuals and businesses are

free to seek economic gain. They may determine the price of their product, make contracts, accumulate capital, and own property.

Economic Concept V

Technological change and invention influences both production and consumption.

Economic Concept VI

Money is a medium of exchange, a measure of value, and a store of value.

Economic Concept VII

Community goods and services are produced by the government. Individuals pay for government goods and services through taxes.

Grade two

Economic Concept I

Satisfying people's wants for goods and services is the end purpose of economic activity. It is what economics is all about.

Economic Concept II

Consumers' demands for desired goods and services basically determine what is produced.

Economic Concept III

Economic activity for the most part depends upon private business firms.

Economic Concept IV

Business firms combine the productive resources of land or natural resources, labor, and capital goods to produce desired goods and services. In our system, most business firms are privately owned.

Economic Concept V

There is a continuous flow of money payments from consumers to business firms in exchange for consumer goods and services and from business firms to workers in exchange for their productive services.

Economic Concept VI

The entrepreneur assumes both responsibility and risk for the business operation. The objective of any private business is to earn profit for its owner or owners. Those products will be produced whose cost of production relative to price returns the highest profit.

Economic Concept VII

Banks produce the financial services needed by individuals and businesses in a community.

Economic Concept VIII

The production of capital goods, buildings, tools, and materials from savings is necessary for the establishment and growth of business firms.

Economic Concept IX
Specialization, or division of labor, increases the efficiency of production and increases interdependence.

Economic Concept X
Technological change, mechanization, and invention influence both production and consumption.

Economic Concept XI
Enforcing rules for the general good and producing certain goods and services are some of the functions of government.

Grade three

Economic Concept I
The basic economic problem confronting all people is the conflict between unlimited wants and limited resources. Individual wants change with time but, collectively, wants are always increasing and unsatisfied.

Economic Concept II
Each country possesses a stock of productive resources. These resources are combined to produce the goods and services the people want.

Economic Concept III
The quantity and quality of the goods and services an economy can produce depend on the quantity and quality of its productive resources, the extent of specialization, and technological progress.

Economic Concept IV
If people are to specialize they must also be able to exchange what they produce for what other people produce. This is done by buying and selling in markets. A market may be local, regional, national, or worldwide.

Economic Concept V
International trade takes place because people in one country need and want what people in other countries produce.

Grade four

Economic Concept I
Economics is the study of the human activities concerned with the creation of goods and services to satisfy human wants.

Economic Concept II
Consumers' demands for each product depend upon their preferences for it relative to competing products, the level of consumer income, and the price of the particular product relative to what alternative purchases might cost.

Economic Concept III
The supply of a product is the total quantity offered for sale in the market by all producers.

Economic Concept IV
The prices of most goods and services in the United States are determined by the interaction of supply and demand in the market.

Economic Concept V
Competition in the market promotes the most efficient use of scarce resources, encourages economic progress, provides individuals with opportunities for self-advancement in business, and benefits the consumer.

Economic Concept VI
The production and marketing of most goods and services is organized and carried on by private firms.

Economic Concept VII
Our American method of making basic economic decisions with respect to the use of productive resources through the system of markets and prices provides us with the maximum amount of economic freedom. Of course, economic freedom—like political freedom —is not absolute. It is limited by certain economic and legal circumstances.

Grade five

Economic Concept I
Each society develops an economic system to deal with the problem of deciding how to allocate limited resources among alternative uses. Economic systems differ among different countries and at different times in history.

Economic Concept II
In our private enterprise system, consumer demand in the market is the main force that allocates the productive resources among competing wants. When resources are used to satisfy one want they cannot be used for something else. Thus, the real cost of the goods and services produced is the value of the things that are foregone.

Economic Concept III
The productive resources a country possesses affect the amount and kind of goods and services that are produced. The quality and quantity of the productive resources change due to discovery, population growth, education, technological progress, and capital formation.

Economic Concept IV
Technological progress refers to the application of new ideas, knowledge, or inventions to economic activities. It may be in the form of discoveries of new supplies or uses of natural resources, new machines, materials, or production methods, or the invention or improvement of consumer goods and services. Technological progress has contributed to the economic growth of our country by increasing the productivity of labor. It also has a profound effect on the ways in

which people work, the amount of income they earn, their level of living, and their way of living.

Economic Concept V

An economic system develops economic institutions to carry on the everyday economic activities of the community. We have such institutions as the use of money and credit, banks, business organizations, labor organizations, and collective bargaining.

Economic Concept VI

Although our private enterprise system is based on decentralized decision making, the government's economic role has increased as our economy has become more complex.

Grade six

Economic Concept I

All societies face the economic problem of deciding how to allocate scarce resources. Some economies rely primarily on the market mechanism, with a restricted role for the government, while others rely heavily on centralized decision-making.

Economic Concept II

All countries want economic growth, that is, increasing their per capita output of goods and services. The main factors affecting the economic growth of a country are the quality and quantity of the productive resources and technological progress.

Economic Concept III

Economically underdeveloped countries usually provide only a low standard of living for their people. The people of these countries want economic growth but are hindered by, among other things, their lack of labor skills and capital resources.

Economic Concept IV

The United States has economic, political, and moral reasons for helping the underdeveloped countries achieve economic growth.

Economic Concept V

Specialization and exchange among nations increase the total quantity of wanted goods and services that can be produced with a given supply of productive resources.[16]

Next, the guide presents the concepts in the children's interpretation with activities for development of the concepts. Supplementary activities and a bibliography of suggested references are included at the end of each grade-level section. At the kindergarten level, "Economic Concept II" is presented with the following activities:

[16]Northwest Council for Economic Education, *Economic Education for Washington Schools, K-6* (Olympia, Washington: Office of State Superintendent of Public Instruction, 1966), pp. xiii–xix.

ECONOMIC CONCEPT II, KINDERGARTEN

All people are confronted with the conflict between unlimited wants and limited resources.

CHILDREN'S INTERPRETATION	ACTIVITIES
Everyone wants many things.	Play a wishing game. Discuss
	What toy would you want if you could have anything?
	Make pictures or stand-up cutouts of these toys. Display them on a bulletin board.
No one can have all the things he wants.	Point out that there are many times at home and at school when one cannot have all he wants of something:
	If one member of the family eats all the dessert he wants, there will not be enough for others in the family.
	If mother buys all the toys the children want, there will not be enough money for food.
	If one child uses up all the easel paint, others cannot paint pictures.
	If one child plays with a school ball (blocks, puzzles) all the time, others do not have a turn to enjoy it.
	If you spend all your time in school making a picture, you do not have time to listen to stories, sing songs, or play games.
Each of us must make choices.	Discuss activities at school that require making choices:

Choosing work period activities.
Selecting art materials from a limited supply.

See *Supplementary Activities* 1 and 2 for kindergarten on pages 9 and 10.

Families must decide what things are most important for them to have.

Discuss choices that must be made by families:

A family must have a home, food, and clothing.

Families must decide whether they will buy things now or save for something they want later.

Story:
Vaughan, Sam, *New Shoes*

Because we cannot have all the things we want, we can better fill our needs and wants if we use the things we do have carefully.

Collect used or scrap items that could be discarded such as an empty box, a piece of construction paper, or a piece of crayon.

Discuss ways these items could be used so we may have more pictures than if these materials were thrown away. Note that we cannot just take more art materials when we want them because materials for each child are limited.

Discuss caring for personal property so it will last longer.

Stories:
Slobodkin, L., *Too Many Mittens*
Kay, Helen, *One Mitten Lewis*

See *Supplementary Activity 3* for kindergarten on page 11.[17]

[17] *Economic Education for Washington Schools, K-6,* pp. 3–4.

87

One of the supplementary activities for "Economic Concept II" follows:

SUPPLEMENTARY ACTIVITIES

ECONOMIC CONCEPT II, KINDERGARTEN—*Supplementary Activity No. 1*

Tell a story about going to the toy store. Have the children act out the action of the story as it is told. Give the children an opportunity to contribute their ideas. For example:

"I am waking up in the morning and now I am jumping out of bed. Today is a special day, I am five years old! I'll get dressed and hurry to breakfast."

"The mailman has brought a special card from Grandmother. And here is another surprise—one dollar! Grandmother wants me to choose a special toy. Mother says I may put on my coat and go to the store now." (Walk, skip, and jump to the store.)

"I want to see all the toys in the store. I see a wagon but it costs two dollars. Can I get the wagon? Here is a doll. It costs one dollar. Can I get the doll? But I like the book, too. It is one dollar. Can I get both the doll and the book? (Have each child select the toy he wants that costs one dollar.) I must give the clerk my dollar and he will wrap the toy. Now I will go home." (Have the children skip and run home.)

Follow-up discussion of the story:

Could you choose *any* toy in the store?

Could you have as *many* toys as you wanted?

Can grown-ups buy *all* the things they want?[18]

The remaining concepts for kindergarten and the other grade levels are presented in the same manner.

Another example of a multidisciplinary program is the Anthropology Program from the University of Georgia, discussed in chapter two.

Interdisciplinary Program

The Greater Cleveland Social Science Program is an example of an interdisciplinary approach to the social sciences. The program for grades 1–6 contains a number of units to be developed at each grade level. Concepts from each of the social science disciplines contribute to the total program, but selected concepts form the basis for each unit. *The*

[18]*Economic Education for Washington Schools, K-6*, p. 9.

Teachers' Guide for the Primary Grades K-2 explains, "In a sequential program, such as GCSSP, the deepening and broadening of conceptual understandings are the links in the chain which binds the content at one grade level to the content of the whole program."[19]

The concepts from each of the disciplines are listed in the guide with the caution that they are not to be treated as a rigid, immutable framework, because some concepts are interdisciplinary.[20] The guide explains, "while we must use the disciplines in exploring concepts, we should not regard the concepts in all cases as elements locked in a strait jacket of one particular discipline."[21]

The units presented for grade 1 are: Review of Concepts Developed in Kindergarten, Map and Globe Skills, Transportation in the United States, A Trip to the Capital of Our Country, Allegiance to My Country, Stories About Great Americans Including George Washington, Abraham Lincoln, Clara Barton, and Amos Fortune.

Unit III in grade 1, Transportation in the United States, lists the major disciplinary concepts to be developed:

MAJOR DISCIPLINARY CONCEPTS FOR UNIT III

Economics

Transportation is essential to trade and to the most efficient division of labor.

Division of labor is the key to efficiency. For best results, work must be divided so that each person can become increasingly expert at his job.

The interdependence of our society is very complicated; it is important to realize that millions of people work to serve, feed, clothe, and house one another.

Production is divided between goods and services. Services tend to bulk larger and larger in advanced economies.

It is important to consider which goods or services are best provided by private and which by public means.

Sociology-Anthropology

A society consists of individuals and groups in constant interaction.

Geography

Geography is concerned with circulation, which includes the movement of people and goods, and with spatial relationships.

The ability to locate places on maps and globes is a skill essential to the study of geography.

[19]Educational Research Council of Greater Cleveland, *Teachers' Guide: Learning About Our Country* (Cleveland: GCSSP/1, I (1966), xi.

[20]*Teachers' Guide*, p. xiii.

[21]*Teachers' Guide*, p. xiii.

One of the many duties of government is to make laws regulating transportation.

Government encourages transportation by subsidies and payments raised by taxation.[22]

A sample page from *The Teachers' Guide for the Primary Grades K-2* on Land Transportation—Trains lists the objectives and the experiences designed to meet these objectives.

OBJECTIVES

TO LEARN THAT PEOPLE
AND FREIGHT ARE CAR-
RIED BY TRAINS

Vocabulary
passenger train
engine and/or
locomotive
freight train
conductor
engineer
railroad track

See Resources for a list of
books about trains. The list
is by no means comprehensive,
but the books included have
clear illustrations of the most
common types of freight cars
and may be helpful in answering questions which may be
posed by pupils.

TO LEARN THAT SOME
TRAINS ARE SPECIALLY
EQUIPPED TO CARRY
PASSENGERS

EXPERIENCES

FILMSTRIP

Railway Transportation (see Resources): This filmstrip may be used
to introduce the study of train
transportation. Nan lives on a farm
near railroad tracks. She likes to
watch trains pass by, carrying
freight and passengers. One day
Nan has a train ride. She learns
about passenger train cars and the
work of the conductor, engineer,
fireman, road repair crews, mail
clerks, and others.

Suggested Questions

What is the difference between a
freight train and a passenger train?

What were some things the freight
train carried?

What special kinds of cars are there
in a passenger train?

Who were some of the workers
mentioned in the filmstrip? What
did they do?

OBSERVATION—DISCUSSION

Examine and discuss pictures and
models of passenger and freight
trains. Include pictures showing
several different types of freight
cars and the interiors of special

[22]*Teachers' Guide*, p. 90.

passenger cars: coach, pullman, diner, railway post office, observation-lounge. Ask pupils to tell about experiences riding trains, or merely seeing them pass by. Mention safety precautions in connection with railroad crossings.

PICTURE STUDY: PASSENGER TRAINS

If the filmstrip was used as suggested, instead of explaining the pictures in the *Pupil Textbook*, the teacher may wish to have pupils tell what they know about the trains and workers illustrated.

Explanations given here for each textbook page should be discussed in addition to questions.

Pupil Textbook, pages 13–17.

Page 13. "Passenger Train." Explain that this is a picture of a passenger train that can carry people on long trips to many places in our country; it also carries passengers' baggage and mail. It has special cars for sitting, eating, sleeping. It has a railway post office car where workers sort mail as the train travels from city to city. Trains travel fast, but not so fast as airplanes. Compare the passenger train with the rapid transit train: How are they the same? Different?[23]

There is a text for pupils with photographs and explanatory captions and sentences to supplement the study. The guide also contains extensive resources.

Advantages and Disadvantages

A program structured in a logical sequential pattern offers the advantage of providing a continuity of experiences. Too often, especially in the primary grades, the social studies program may be a haphazard collection of unrelated experiences. Children thus exposed to a wide variety of experiences may not develop an understanding of the social sciences as disciplines or of their methods of inquiry.

In a sequential program, the children's maturity level is considered to determine the placement of concepts at levels where most children

[23]*Teachers' Guide*, p. 116.

will be able to comprehend them. This consideration prevents the presentation of concepts too difficult for the majority of children at a given level.

Disadvantages of the structured program include its failure to include incidents and problems that arise within the children's environment. Interrupting the sequential pattern to pursue an unrelated topic breaks the continuity of the program. Another suggested disadvantage is the program's failure to meet individual differences within the classroom. Obviously, some children may not have the background of experiences necessary to understand the concepts presented. This situation would be especially prevalent in disadvantaged areas.

SELECTED REFERENCES

Bruner, Jerome S., *The Process of Education.* New York: Random House, Inc., 1960.

Conceptual Framework: Social Studies. Madison: Wisconsin State Department of Education, 1967.

Ford, G. W., and Lawrence Pugno, eds., *The Structure of Knowledge and the Curriculum.* Chicago: Rand McNally & Co., 1964.

Joyce, Bruce R., *Strategies for Elementary Social Science Education.* Chicago: Science Research Associates, Inc., 1965.

Morrissett, Irving, ed., *Concepts and Structure in the New Social Science Curricula.* West Lafayette, Indiana: Social Science Education Consortium, 1966.

Price, Ray A., Warren Hickman, and Gerald Smith, *Major Concepts for Social Studies.* Syracuse: Social Studies Curriculum Center, Syracuse University, 1966.

Schwab, Joseph J., "The Concept of the Structure of a Discipline," *Educational Record,* XLIII (July, 1962), 197–205.

Womack, James G., *Discovering the Structure of Social Studies.* New York: Benziger Press, 1966.

CHAPTER SIX

Teaching the Disadvantaged

A DISCUSSION OF TEACHING THE DISADVANTAGED IS INCLUDED in the methodology section of this book because of the many special considerations in terms of content, teaching techniques, and classroom conditions that must be used for disadvantaged children. These special considerations do, in fact, formulate a method.

Hundreds of thousands of disadvantaged children enter classrooms each day. These children are found in large numbers in inner-city schools; they are frequently encountered in lower-income and rural schools; and a few are scattered throughout almost any school in the nation. Many a child would call himself disadvantaged simply because he did not receive that bicycle he wanted or because his family doesn't own color television. Unfortunately, the disadvantaged referred to here are not so lucky. They are those children who were deprived "of the same opportunity for healthy growth and development as is available to the vast majority."[1] These disadvantaged children do not possess the needed skills to be successful in school. Most of these children come from homes with chaotic environments; they have not engaged in effective verbal interaction with adults at important developmental stages; and they have had few experiences outside their homes. How does one identify a disadvantaged child?

In recent years, these children have worn many labels. They have been referred to as "culturally deprived," "culturally disadvantaged," "underprivileged," and "from low socioeconomic backgrounds." It is important for teachers to realize, however, that the disadvantaged label does not indicate a specific subculture, color, or socioeconomic level. Granted, concentrations of the disadvantaged may be found in minority groups and in areas of low socioeconomic levels, but it is incorrect to label all children from these groups as such. It is also incorrect to assume that disadvantaged children are not to be found in affluent majority groups.

An accurate description of disadvantaged children is difficult because so many factors contributed to the condition. Larson and Olson identify disadvantaged children as follows:

1. Language development—underdeveloped expressive and receptive skills as well as speech patterns which conflict with dominant language norms.
2. Self-concept—inadequate self-image which will lead to self-doubt and insecurity resulting in low school achievement and a lessened feeling of personal worth.
3. Social skills—possess a minimal amount of skill in conventional manners and social amenities; unskilled in relating socially to peers and authority figures; and unable to function effectively in school group.
4. Cultural differences—most come from lower income and minority groups and will possess beliefs and behaviors which may differ from dominant groups in school.[2]

Special teaching methods are required for disadvantaged children to compensate for their inadequacies in school. The following pertinent methods are found to be effective:

The provision of cues which are salient and concrete, the ensuring of direct participation in the learning situation by every child, and the reinforcement of correct or desired responses. . .[3]

[1]Jerome Hellmuth, ed., *Disadvantaged Child* (Seattle: Special Child Publications, 1967), p. 21.
[2]Staten W. Webster, ed., *The Disadvantaged Learner: Knowing, Understanding, Educating* (San Francisco, Calif.: Chandler Publishing Co., 1966), p. 491.
[3]Sophia Bloom, "Improving the Education of Culturally Deprived Children: Applying Learning Theory to Classroom Instruction," *Chicago School Journal*, XLV (December, 1963), 126–31.

Disadvantaged children have been present since schools were established, but our current increasing population and our lack of appropriate compensatory programs has created a tremendous educational and social problem. Impetus for alleviating this problem has been provided by federal monies directed toward improving educational programs for the disadvantaged. This effort, however, may be too little too late. Unless individual teachers accept the responsibility for adapting their educational programs to the needs of the disadvantaged, a generous portion of the potential talent of our nation will be lost.

Complicating the problems of the disadvantaged is the fact that teachers find it difficult to teach these children. Teachers with years of experience repeatedly "transfer out" of the difficult schools. The reasons most often given for transfer requests have been identified as the teacher's incompatibility with the "personality peculiarities" of the disadvantaged.[4] Teachers who have a basic sympathy for the disadvantaged and a conviction that these children must not be rejected because of their "cultural peculiarities" must be selected.[5] How can teachers with these qualities be selected?

Research conducted with a group of student teachers found that the use of a "Cultural Attitude Inventory" was significant. To select student teachers who were successful with the disadvantaged, the inventory required reactions to statements such as:

Children from disadvantaged homes need socialization experiences, but time in school should not be wasted on these experiences.

Disadvantaged children should not be given help, but be taught as other children.

Teachers should respect disadvantaged children rather than pity or love them.[6]

To be effective with the disadvantaged, teachers need the crucial ingredient of a basic human respect[7] along with a sense of idealism, dedication to a cause, and a desire to help the "have-nots" and to render service.

Children from disadvantaged backgrounds have been characterized as the most difficult group to teach, because they lack learning ability, outside training, and interest in schooling.[8] Teachers find three basic

[4]Patrick J. Groff, "Dissatisfaction in Teaching the CD Child," *Phi Delta Kappan*, XLV (November, 1963), 76.

[5]Groff, "Dissatisfaction in Teaching the CD Child," p. 76.

[6]Dorothy J. Skeel, "Determining the Compatibility of Student Teachers for Culturally Deprived Areas by Means of a Cultural Attitude Inventory" (Doctoral Dissertation, Pennsylvania State University, 1966).

[7]Frank Riessman and A. Hannah, "Big-City School: Problems and Prospects," *Parent Teacher Magazine*, LIX (November, 1964), 14.

[8]Howard S. Becker, "Social Class Variations in the Teacher-Pupil Relationship," *Journal of Educational Sociology*, XXV (April, 1952), 452–54.

problems in their adjustment to teaching these children: (1) presenting learning experiences, (2) discipline, (3) moral acceptability. These students do not meet the specifications of the "perfect student," and the usual teaching techniques are inadequate. However, disadvantaged children indicate a natural responsiveness to a person who reacts favorably toward them; they demonstrate a keen desire to be noticed and respected as persons, and they have a general liking for school.[9]

Another imposing problem of working with the disadvantaged is the lack of materials specifically designed to meet their needs. A book that describes the pleasantries of a middle-class white family, where Daddy goes to work every day and Mom stays home with the children, has little appeal for the child living in a ghetto. Or, the social studies book that discusses community helpers such as the butcher, the library lady, and the policeman provides little interest for the child whose world is filled with welfare workers, attendance officers, and probation people.

The teacher of the disadvantaged, whether all the members of his class or only one or two fit the label, faces a number of challenges: (1) possessing and exhibiting the proper attitude toward these children, (2) compensating for their learning problems, (3) selecting appropriate materials or preparing them if acceptable ones are not available, and (4) adjusting teaching techniques to coincide with learning styles. These challenges are present no matter what the subject area. Possibly, the challenges are even more demanding in the social studies because the concepts developed are so dependent on the extent of previous experiences.

Objectives

Social studies objectives for the disadvantaged are formulated with consideration for their learning problems and environmental factors. Broad general objectives include:

Acquire knowledge:

Of the history of minority groups and their contributions to the cultural heritage of the nation.

Of the child's immediate environment in order to enable him to understand its relationship to the larger world.

Of the democratic process and the importance of the individual assuming his responsibility.

[9]Skeel, "Determining the Compatibility of Student Teachers," p. 80.

Acquire an understanding:

Of the contribution that each individual makes to the group of which he is a member.

Of the reasons why prejudice occurs and its effect on society and the relationships of people.

Of the problems of poverty and prejudice that occur in other cultures of the world.

Of the relationship of what is learned in school to the child's everyday activities.

To develop an attitude:

Of the worth of each individual as a member of society.

Of the value of learning and its potential to provide a better future for each child.

Develop skill:

In communicating with others through oral and written methods.

In getting along with others in the immediate group and in society.

In acquiring information through critical reading, listening, and observing.

These objectives vary in accordance with the specific needs and background of the group. The emphasis here is placed on the necessity for experiences in social studies to compensate for the disadvantages the child brings to school with him.

Obviously, most of the problems the disadvantaged child faces as he enters school are the result of deprivation in his early formative years. Nursery and "Headstart" programs are aimed at attempting to alleviate some of this deprivation. However, the child still enters school disadvantaged in the areas previously outlined. His future appears quite different to him than it does to the average child. He sees little offered by the traditional school that applies to his life. Therefore, teachers must adapt their programs to meet the needs and interests of these children. What adaptations are necessary?

Before planning educational programs, the teacher would be wise to investigate common conditions in the experiences of disadvantaged groups that have contributed to their present situation. These factors, however, are not to be used as excuses for lack of success with disadvantaged children; rather, they should increase the teacher's understanding of their problems.

Most of these children come from large families, which precipitate crowded living conditions, limited parental attention, and excessive inappropriate stimuli such as shouting, crying, and loud radio or TV playing. The children's parents lack education and social know-how, are often unemployed or in low-paying unskilled jobs, move frequently, and perpetuate these same conditions in their children.

The discipline exhibited in the home is often of a physical nature, authoritative, inconsistent, and immediate to alleviate a present situation as soon as possible. Patriarchal authority reigns in the home with the exception of the Negro family, which is most often dominated by the mother.

Children are given responsibilities early—for example, the care of younger children or particular household chores. This tendency results in less concern for self and more group orientation. Early independence gives way to peer domination, which replaces the family as a socializing agent and source of values.[10] Frequent illness and lack of proper food, health, and dental care decrease the children's efficiency as learners.

Equally important and, as Riessman points out, possibly more important are some of the positives of the culture of the disadvantaged. Riessman feels that some of these positives are an interest in vocational education; parents' and children's respect for education in spite of their dislike for school where they sense a resentment toward them; the children's slow cognitive style of learning, hidden verbal talent, freedom from self-blame and parental overprotection, lack of sibling rivalry, informality, humor, and enjoyment of music, games, and sports.[11] These positives may provide a basis on which teachers can build a more adequate educational program.

Initially, experiences offered these children should be vital and motivational. They should build upon the children's present background. First, the children should be re-introduced to their immediate environment and helped to understand it. Then, their horizons should be expanded to a wider environment. Have the children ever been on a bus, gone to the super market, visited a museum, baked cookies, had someone really listen while they talked, or experienced approval upon completion of a task?

"Bereiter and Engelmann claim that enriching experiences are not enough. They claim that the disadvantaged do not have enough time to participate in the same experiences as privileged children. Therefore, selection and exclusion of experiences is necessary to provide those activities which will produce a faster than normal rate of progress."[12] Their discussion is primarily aimed at a preschool program; however, it certainly should be considered when planning programs at any level.

Cultural deprivation is synonymous with language deprivation. It is

[10]A. Harry Passow, ed., *Education in Depressed Areas* (New York: Teachers College Publications, 1963), p. 113.

[11]Frank Riessman, "The Culturally Deprived Child: A New View," *School Life*, XLV (April, 1963), 57.

[12]Carl Bereiter and Siegfried Engelmann, *Teaching Disadvantaged Children in the Preschool* (Englewood Cliffs, N.J.: Prentice-Hall, Inc., 1966), pp. 6–19.

apparent that the disadvantaged child has mastered a language "that is adequate for maintaining social relationships and for meeting his social and material needs, but he does not learn how to use language for obtaining and transmitting information, for monitoring his own behavior, and for carrying on verbal reasoning."[13] The disadvantaged child cannot use language "to explain, to describe, to instruct, to inquire, to hypothesize, to analyze, to compare, to deduce, and to test."[14] If such language deprivation has not been corrected by the time the child enters the formal school, it certainly should affect the approach used for teaching social studies.

Research indicates that the following factors should be considered in planning educational programs for the disadvantaged: (1) children's interest and concern for the here and now; (2) extensive concrete examples are necessary for their cognitive style of perception and learning; (3) the children experience difficulty in classifying, relating, and integrating knowledge; (4) learning is most successful when the process is self-involving and of an active nature; (5) the teacher should show an expectation of success; (6) repetition of information is necessary through a variety of approaches; and (7) there should be continuous feedback to the student on his progress.[15]

CONDITIONS OF THE CLASSROOM

More than any other single factor, the importance of an interesting and stimulating classroom cannot be stressed too much. Children need to feel that the classroom is a place where they will learn and where they are respected as individuals, not rejected because they have problems. Examples of some items that should be included in the environment are small animals such as a rabbit, snake, or bird or a plant. Such items present the children with an opportunity to learn to care for and be responsible for living things, which are often not a part of their world. Pictures of people and places within the community should be used to permit children to identify school with the outside world. Books, books, books at varying levels of difficulty and containing stories of experiences related to and expanding upon the child's experiences are needed. Vast amounts of concrete materials and visual aids are necessary. Equally important is the provision for the children to share the responsibility of the upkeep of the classroom.

[13]Bereiter and Engelmann, *Teaching Disadvantaged Children in the Preschool*, p. 42.

[14]Bereiter and Engelmann, *Teaching Disadvantaged Children in the Preschool*, p. 31.

[15]Webster, ed., *The Disadvantaged Learner*, p. 477.

ROLE OF THE TEACHER

Crucial to the success of disadvantaged children in school is the presence of a teacher who can be trusted. The teacher must understand and be sincerely interested in the children's problems. He must be cognizant of the most effective teaching techniques for these children. Also, he must be willing to accept the children as they are and help them learn as much as possible.

Teachers with middle-class backgrounds will need to learn about the culture of the disadvantaged and about how to work cooperatively with the parents to achieve the best results. The teacher is an important link between the home and the school. He should never discredit the values, beliefs, and customs of the culture of the disadvantaged; yet, he should offer the children an awareness of another way of life. Parents are interested in the practical value of schooling for their children, and they should be made to feel welcome and involved in school activities.

A tremendous responsibility is placed on the teacher, since motivation for learning is often lacking in the disadvantaged. Generally, such motivation can be accomplished by a responsive teacher using carefully selected materials, methods, and topics.

Selection of Content

As pointed out previously, there are certain factors inherent in the social studies that are not as problematic in other subject areas. Webster relates the following: "the content in social studies is of highly verbal nature—more reading is required than in almost any other subject; topics are frequently removed from realities of life chronologically and spatially; and many of the values, attitudes, and behaviors advocated are contrary to those of the disadvantaged."[16] Also, the materials available portray experiences that are often remote from the lives of the disadvantaged. An awareness of these factors will permit teachers to compensate for them. Considering the learning problems of the disadvantaged as well as the problems inherent in the social studies, what should be included in the content of the social studies program?

The goal of such a program is for the disadvantaged to learn the same basic concepts of social studies as any elementary-school child; however, adaptation will be necessary to relate the content to their everyday lives.

[16]Webster, ed., *The Disadvantaged Learner*, p. 586.

The following model serves as a basis for planning programs for the disadvantaged, whether they be urban or rural oriented.

IMMEDIATE ENVIRONMENT	REMOVED ENVIRONMENT

Kindergarten—Grade 1

His home, family, and school—Discussion centers on the type of family relationships that occur in the environment of the child—an example might be the presence of different adults in the home such as aunts, uncles, grandmothers, etc. or the absence of a father. No attempt should be made to place emphasis on the typical mother-father-child relationship of the middle-class home. To develop the self-concept, stress should be placed on the individual and his role.	Select a culture that has a similar family relationship—for example, have the Mexican-American learn Mexican customs.
Local community—Stress available libraries, museums, parks, recreation areas, and community services.	
Important people—Discuss leaders in the community and nation but, most important, select leaders from the children's culture such as Martin Luther King for Negro children.	

Grade 2

Democratic processes—Discuss the problems of a minority, using those apparent within the classroom, for example, the failure to choose a favorite game or the presence of more girls than boys.	Group minority problems in national relationship.
National heritage—Stress contributions of their particular culture such as music, art.	Symbols such as flag, holidays, freedom.
Economic concepts—Work in the family, neighborhood, school. Study problems of lack of money, resources, unemployment.	Other areas of the nation with similar problems.

IMMEDIATE ENVIRONMENT (*continued*)   REMOVED ENVIRONMENT (*continued*)

Grade 3

Historical—Choose a local memorial, monument, or early settlement of the area.

Early pioneers, Indians, people who came from lands specific to the group's ancestry.

Relationship of urban and rural areas—Children in rural setting learn about their contributions to cities in terms of food, labor, purchases; children in the city learn of their contributions to the country.

Cities or rural areas beyond local environment.

Communication—Within the classroom, use methods beyond spoken language, e.g., facial expressions, actions.

Systems including different languages relating to their cultural background.

Transportation—Stress modes used in their community and the problems presented.

Link to previous study of cities and their available modes of transportation.

Grade 4

Geographic concepts of locale—Study climate, rainfall, and terrain.

Similar geographic conditions in other areas of the world.

Contrasting geographic conditions existing in close proximity to the local environment and in other parts of the world.

Social, economic, and political problems of the community.

National and world problems of a similar nature.

Grade 5

Governmental processes—Begin with class organization, school, and community.

State and national government —and relation to early development —birth of the nation.

Contrasting governments.

Local racial or nationality problems.

Discuss the Civil War, Spanish-American War, etc. to help the children understand the possible origins of their problems.

Grade 6

Family background of children in classroom.

Nations of children's ancestors.

Neighboring community's ancestral background.

United Nations.

This model does not provide an exhaustive list of the content to be included in the social studies, nor are the grade lines intended to be restrictive. The model attempts to show a pattern of relationships between the concerns of the immediate environment and the removed environment. This model stresses the necessity of beginning with the here and now and expanding to that which is distant and past.

Special Instructional Considerations

Adaptation of the content is important, but it is not sufficient to allow the disadvantaged learner to receive maximum benefit from the instruction. Other necessary considerations involve organizational patterns, teaching methods, activities, and materials.[17]

ORGANIZATIONAL PATTERNS

The organization of the class affects subject areas other than the social studies, and it is an important consideration. Team teaching has been used successfully with disadvantaged children.[18] A faculty team comprised of a team leader, four teachers (each with a class), a college intern, and a team mother provides more individualized instruction, increased motivation for learning, different teaching styles, and flexibility in scheduling. Disadvantaged children need the opportunity provided by the team to identify with many adults. Discipline is maintained more readily and neophyte teachers are more effectively introduced to working with disadvantaged children in a team-teaching situation.

Organization based on nongraded continuous progress is beneficial because it removes the failure complex and emphasizes individualization of instruction. Children are grouped by ages; they begin working at their respective levels, and they move ahead as rapidly as possible. Interest grouping across class or grade lines, specifically in social studies, provides increased motivation because children are encouraged to select their own group based on their interest in a topic. Within-class grouping, organized according to specific skills or friendship groups, adds to both the interest and flexibility of the program. Children can learn to work more effectively with others, and they can move freely from group to group.

[17]Helen K. MacKintosh, Lillian Gore, and Gertrude Lewis, *Educating Children in the Middle Grades* (Washington, D.C.: U.S. Department of Health, Education, and Welfare, Office of Education, 1965), p. 39.
[18]MacKintosh, Gore, and Lewis, *Educating Children in the Middle Grades*, p. 39.

TEACHING METHODS

This chapter previously stated that disadvantaged children have difficulty with reasoning and need more concrete experiences to facilitate learning. Teachers must adapt teaching methods to avoid pursuing abstractions without providing concrete examples. It is important for teachers to move from the concrete to the abstract.

The teacher should use open-ended questioning to motivate thinking and to remove the block of the one-right-answer syndrome. Repetitive use of this method is necessary because first experiences may be discouraging.

A variety of approaches to the same topic should be used. Only unlearned content should be repeated. Asubel suggests that material should be thoroughly learned before new material is presented.[19] Disadvantaged children need more guidance from the teacher; however, this guidance should later lead to independent action. Problem solving and unit teaching methods should both be used.

ACTIVITIES

Role-playing is regarded as most effective with the disadvantaged.[20] It permits children to work out a situation physically or to be an active part of an incident.

An increasing number of experiences should be provided for the use of oral language. Verbalization in discussions, role-playing, reporting, and dramatizations is vital. Talking in small groups first will increase the child's confidence in meeting a large group situation. By reading information and stories to the children, the teacher facilitates learning for the disadvantaged reader and increases listening skills. However, care should be exercised to be certain children understand the vocabulary and concepts of what is being read. Concrete materials should be used to illustrate the reading.

Disadvantaged children enjoy games, which should be used when possible and profitable. Excessive competition should be avoided by frequent changing of team membership.

Situations should be provided for children to express their feelings and emotions. Honest appraisal of feelings such as hate, love, distrust, trust, and honesty should be included. These experiences help children understand themselves and others.

---

[19]Webster, ed., *The Disadvantaged Learner*, p. 593.
[20]Fannie R. Shaftel and George Shaftel, *Role-Playing for Social Values: Decision Making in the Social Studies* (Englewood Cliffs, N.J.: Prentice-Hall, Inc., 1967), p. 149.

Experiences in which each child repeatedly meets success are vital to the disadvantaged. Praise and encouragement should be built-in factors of every experience.

MATERIALS

Excessive use of textbooks is unfortunate, for they are often unrelated to the children's experiences and difficult for them in terms of conceptual development and vocabulary usage. The teacher should select materials specifically related to the culture of the child.[21]

Extensive concrete materials and visual aids are necessities for the disadvantaged. Teachers should develop a storehouse of their own materials related to their children's needs.

Role of the Disadvantaged Child in the Classroom

Teachers need to explain the role expected of the child in the learning situation. This explanation has frequently not been accomplished by the home environment. The child must first be motivated to learn. By showing that he expects the child to be successful, the teacher assists him in building a good self-concept. As the child gains confidence, he becomes less dependent on the teacher. As he becomes involved in learning activities, his interest increases. Hopefully, he then understands his role as a learner.

The environment should be more structured in the beginning in order that the child may learn the advantages of organized behavior. Freedom of decisions and choices can be permitted as he learns self-discipline.

Advantages of Teaching the Disadvantaged

A rather obvious advantage is the increased interest and motivation on the part of the disadvantaged child. Higher achievement levels can be expected, and a decrease in the dreadful waste of the disadvantaged child's potential can be achieved.

[21]Jean D. Grambs, *Methods and Materials in Intergroup Education: Annotated and Selected Bibliography* (College Park, Maryland: University of Maryland, 1967).

Difficulties involved in teaching the disadvantaged include the need for increased commitment and dedication on the part of the teacher. Any child will progress when nurtured in an environment of respect and understanding, but the disadvantaged child needs even more. He needs enough time, energy, and money expended upon him to enable him to develop the full potential of his ability.

It might be argued that the methods and materials discussed in this chapter would be advantageous to any child. This argument is probably true, but for the disadvantaged child, these methods are a necessity.

SELECTED REFERENCES

Bereiter, Carl and Siegfried Englemann, *Teaching Disadvantaged Children in the Preschool*. Englewood Cliffs, N.J.: Prentice-Hall, Inc., 1966.

Grambs, Jean D., *Methods and Materials in Intergroup Education: Annotated and Selected Bibliography*. College Park, Maryland: University of Maryland, 1967.

Hickerson, Nathaniel, *Education for Alienation*. Englewood Cliffs, N.J.: Prentice-Hall, Inc., 1966.

Kozol, Jonathan, *Death At An Early Age*. Boston: Houghton Mifflin Company, 1967.

Moore, G. Alexander, *Realities of the Urban Classroom: Observations in the Elementary Schools*. New York: Frederick A. Praeger, Inc., 1967.

Passow, A. Harry, Miriam Goldberg, and Abraham J. Tannebaum, eds., *Education of the Disadvantaged*. New York: Holt, Rinehart & Winston, Inc., 1967.

Riessman, Frank, *The Culturally Deprived Child*. New York: Harper & Row, Publishers, 1962.

Taba, Hilda and Deborah Elkins, *Teaching Strategies of the Culturally Disadvantaged*. New York: Rand McNally & Co., 1966.

Warner, Sylvia Ashston, *The Teacher*. New York: Simon and Schuster, Inc., 1963.

Webster, Staten W., ed., *The Disadvantaged Learner: Knowing, Understanding, Educating*. San Francisco, Calif.: Chandler Publishing Co., 1966.

Does the solution to many of our current problems rest with an informed and concerned citizenry?

PART THREE

Selected Content
for Emphasis

THE NATIONAL AND INTERNATIONAL PROBLEMS FACING OUR country today require that particular emphasis be placed on teaching current affairs and international understandings in our elementary schools. If children are to be active participants assuming the responsibility that citizenship affords them, they should begin early to be knowledgeable about the events occurring around them. Controversial issues should be presented with an open-minded attitude. All sides of an issue must be viewed, and children should be encouraged to take a position on the issue in question. Only through intelligent critically-thinking citizens will we find solutions to our domestic and foreign problems.

Our world has grown too small, due to our fast transportation systems, to allow us to be unfamiliar with the culture and customs of people around the world. The close contacts of all peoples today require that children build an understanding of cultures different from their own and an appreciation of the similarities of all peoples. In their home or community environment, children are often exposed to unfavorable attitudes toward other cultures. Consequently, the school must assume the responsibility of fostering better relationships among men.

This section discusses the rationale behind teaching current affairs and international understandings and presents activities that can be initiated for the development of these topics.

CHAPTER SEVEN

Teaching Current Affairs

NUMEROUS PURPOSES CAN BE LISTED FOR TEACHING AN elementary-school child about the daily events occurring around him; however, none is so pressing as the need for helping each child become a knowledgeable citizen—one who is an interested and active participant in the affairs of his world. Perpetuation of our democratic way of living requires the attainment of this goal.

Another vital purpose involves the development of the child's awareness concerning the social and political problems existing in our country. The discrimination against racial and minority groups that causes serious difficulties within many cities and towns, the extreme poverty that deprives people of a decent living, and the differences of opinion in our political parties concerning important issues are only examples of the many problems we face. The early attitudes children develop about these problems and their ability to attempt to solve them are important outcomes of instruction in this area.

Our rapidly changing world affects each child's life. Failure to understand the reasons for and the effects of change is frustrating. Through the study of current affairs, the child becomes aware of and is more willing to accept the changes in his world.

Because our nation is so often affected by events in other parts of the world, children must be aware of the complicated relationships that create these situations. From this understanding, children will become aware of the power wielded by their own and other nations.

Research and discussion of the events occurring in their daily lives permits children to relate school learning to the outside world. They realize that what they are learning aids them in solving their daily problems and provides understanding of others' problems. Children soon begin to realize that history is happening right now and that there is a relationship between past history and current events.

Children, through the study of current affairs, will acquire the habit of reading newspapers, listening to news reports, and discussing these events with others. This habit should be retained throughout adult life. The children will find it difficult to completely understand many of the items they hear about or read about, and it is important to discuss and clarify these topics. The children will also sharpen their skills in critical reading, looking at all sides of an issue, evaluating the source of information, oral language (through reporting and discussion), vocabulary, recognizing propaganda techniques, recognizing important news events, and summarizing news reports.

Objectives for teaching current affairs are:

To develop knowledgeable active citizens of the community, nation, and world.

To develop an awareness of the tremendous social and political problems of our nation.

To facilitate the understanding of the nature of change.

To appreciate the position of the United States as a power in the world community.

To increase the relationship of school learning to the everyday world.

To increase proficiency in the language art skills of critical reading, thinking, evaluating, oral language, vocabulary, and summarizing.

When to Start

As soon as children come to school, they should be introduced to the current events within their understanding. Teachers can start with reports of events in the children's lives as an introduction. The first concept to be learned is that events make news. The next step is to learn what news is important. Many teachers start the day with the development of a class newspaper containing items from the children's lives. After the children have developed an understanding of what a newspaper should contain, items are included from other rooms in the school, the community, nation, and world. An example of what such a newspaper might contain follows:

> Today is October 24, 19___.
> The weather is warm and sunny.
>
> Sharon Gray's house burned last night.
> It is located at 24 Locust Street.
>
> Shadyside School will hold an Ice Cream Social. It will be Wednesday at 8:00 in the evening.
>
> The Riverside Community Park will build a swimming pool. Boys and girls can learn to swim.
>
> National elections will be held next month. Our parents will elect a President of the United States.

Some variations of this activity are: Small groups of children might prepare their own newspaper or draw pictures of current events and discuss them with the class. Teachers can clip pictures from newspapers and magazines and discuss them with the children, who can then develop captions that demonstrate their understanding of the events in the pictures. These pictures also provide display material for the bulletin board.

To provide children with a thorough understanding of events of importance occurring locally, nationally, or in the world, the teacher should plan problem-solving situations or units of study. Examples of such events might be a natural catastrophe such as a flood, tornado, or hurricane; political campaigns; space events; wars and confrontations; and events that relate to past or current topics of study.

Continuation throughout the elementary-school grades of these and other activities concerning current events will foster favorable attitudes toward and natural concern about affairs of the world. The enthusiasm and interest displayed by the teacher are vital factors in the success of these activities.

Suggested Activities

BULLETIN BOARDS

A bulletin board should be reserved for displaying news items or pictures relating to current affairs. An important point to remember is the necessity for frequent changing of its contents. Captions on the board such as "What's New?," "What in the World is Going On?," "News of Our World" stimulate interest.

Division of the board into areas for local, state, national, and international items help children differentiate the news events. The use of a world map on the board enables children to locate the area of the news event and helps them develop map skills. A thread of yarn attached to the location of the event and leading to the written report helps the children associate the place and the event. Responsibility for the bulletin board can be assigned to committees of children or be a dual obligation of the teacher and children.

NEWS REPORTING

A variety of organizational patterns can be used to assign children the responsibility of reporting the news. For example, a child might be assigned the responsibility for the news of one day or one week, or committees of children can be assigned the responsibility for a certain period of time. Tape recording of these reports provides some variety.

The establishment of a mock radio or TV station within the classroom supplies more reality for the news-reporting situation. Special broadcasts or programs can be planned when outstanding events take place. Some classrooms may wish to conduct a daily morning news broadcast with reporters assigned specific areas of the news. Intermediate-grade children may provide the news program for the entire school over the public address system. Included in these programs may be school news of interest to all.

Items for children to remember when reporting the news:

1. Do I understand what is happening in the news event?
2. Can I discuss it with the other children?
3. Do I know enough about it to answer most of the questions the children might ask?
4. Are there any words that I'll need some help in pronouncing?
5. Is the event of interest to most of the children, or will it add knowledge to a topic we are studying?

CLASS NEWSPAPER

The organization of the class into a newspaper staff to publish and distribute a school newspaper provides realistic experience for news reporting. Reporters can be assigned to secure news of the different classes, the school office, and special events. Additional reporters can use outside sources to obtain significant local and national news. Many language skills, as well as social skills, are developed by interviewing people and writing news reports. A sample front page from a school newspaper is shown on p. 116.

The entire school can be organized to prepare the newspaper if an individual class doesn't want to take on the total responsibility. Generally, one of the intermediate grades handles the organization of the paper, and reporters are selected from the other classes.

A field trip to a local newspaper provides background information and increased interest in newspaper publication. If a field trip is not possible, a resource person from the newspaper can visit the classroom to discuss the newspaper with the children.

ROLE-PLAYING, DISCUSSION, AND DEBATES

Role-playing can be used to advantage with news events. It requires that children have a thorough understanding of the event before they attempt to act out the situation for others. Dramatizing a summit meeting or the speech of a famous person helps children realize what the event was like.

Discussions can be organized in many ways. The total class might research a specific topic and attempt to present different points of view, or a news program might be watched on TV—either at school or at home —and discussed. When differences of opinion occur within the group, a debate provides a valuable experience. Both sides can present their views and the children in the class can decide which side presents the best argument. Before the debate takes place, ground rules must be established for time limits on speaking, the use of notes, and the manner of answering the opposition.

READING NEWSPAPERS

The presence of a daily newspaper in the classroom or library is excellent stimulation for developing the habit of reading newspapers. It is also advisable to secure several popular news magazines to complete the resources. Even primary-grade children benefit from the pictures presented.

STOP! LOOK! AND THINK!
by the Sixth Grade

Stop!

Did you know that ice is very dangerous? Well it is! Accidents on ice can cause serious injuries, especially when you are fooling around. If you don't watch out you might break an arm or leg. There have been too many accidents this year because someone wasn't thinking.

Look!

Look where you walk. Be careful where you play. Don't play on ice or very slippery snow. Watch when crossing the street. Don't run.

Let's say that you are walking along and all of a sudden your feet fly up in the air and you are flat on your back. You know it was ice that made you fall, but you didn't see it. Ice is very dangerous in dark and shady places where the light cannot shine on it.

Think!

You just can't stop and look, you have to think! You have a better chance of not getting hurt if you think, so Stop! Look! and Think!

WORLD NEWS

President Johnson gave a State of the Union Address. (A State of the Union Address is a speech given by the President. He gives it to the new Congress every January.)

He talked about continuing programs for fighting poverty in our nation. He stated that taxes could not be cut for this reason. He also discussed the money needed to continue our military help in Vietnam.

FROM THE OFFICE

Dr. Brown is pleased with our assembly programs. He hopes that we will have more assemblies in the next part of the year.

On February 11th and 12th a visitor from Spain will be at our school. Her name is Senorita Maria Asuncion Sole. She is from Barcelona, Spain.

Mere reading of news material without learning to recognize biased presentations and propaganda techniques is useless. The provision of news materials with differing points of view helps children understand how the same news events can be reported differently if the reporters possess opposing viewpoints.

Propaganda techniques such as emotionalized words, vague general statements, name calling, or the band-wagon, testimonial, or plain-folks treatments are examples that elementary-school children can recognize.

Emotionalized words are words that stir very strong feelings within us whenever we hear them. "Loved ones," "mother," "home," "our rights," and "our duties" are examples of words used to blind us with emotion and, thus, distract us from the main point of the discussion. An example of their use might be "Vote for Joe Doakes, he'll protect your home and loved ones." We are so concerned about our home and loved ones that we are willing to vote for Joe Doakes without determining if he has the proper qualifications. Newspapers and magazines use emotionalized words to excite people about reading certain articles. We frequently see headlines such as "Mother Loses Home," "Rights Are Blocked," or "Children Beaten."

Children often use the band-wagon technique to secure permission for something they wish to do—it is the "everyone's doing it, why can't I," trick. It is the idea of following the crowd or jumping on the band wagon to attain a goal.

The testimonial is frequently used in advertising. If such and such a famous person uses a product, then the product must be good for everyone. In politics, too, a candidate supported by an outstanding person gains additional support from the public.

The plain-folks technique is used by politicians. They appear to dress, act, and think like the people from whom they are seeking votes. An example of this technique is the politician who visits the farm, milks the cows, pitches hay, or drives the tractor to convince the people that he is one of them. Actually, he may never have done these things before.

Name calling is used by various individuals and groups to label someone favorably or unfavorably. Many people automatically stop listening to or reading about someone who has been labeled by a name that is unsavory to them. Names such as "communist," "liar," and "traitor" influence people against the individual so labeled. "Good guy," "patriot," and "democrat" are names that may influence a person favorably.

Vague general statements about a topic confuse individuals. Failure to include any proof of a statement's claim makes it difficult to determine its accuracy. "Many politicians are crooked" is an example of a vague general statement.

Children should be able to identify and give examples of the different propaganda techniques, and they should relate this understanding to the material they encounter in newspapers and magazines and on television. Here are some sample statements:

1. *Plain folks.* Sam Arthur, a man of the people, one who came from a humble beginning, is the man for you.
2. *Name Calling.* Joe Doakes is a communist and should not be permitted to run for office.
3. *Testimonial.* Mr. President endorses the candidate John Smith for governor. You'll want to vote for him.
4. *Emotionalized words.* He is a protector of our rights.
5. *Band wagon.* Millions of people use Granny's Glue and so should you.
6. *Vague general statements.* Everyone agrees that new sidewalks are needed in Jonesville.

Controversial Issues

Many a teacher steps lightly for a variety of reasons when issues of controversy arise in the news or classroom. Fear of losing his job, his own prejudice, lack of knowledge of the issue, school policy, community feeling, or a lack of concern are possible causes for a teacher's timidity in this area. Controversial issues, from racial problems to the population explosion, are found in almost every newspaper or newscast. How can they be avoided? Should they be avoided?

Certain controversial issues should be discussed in the elementary school, for children need the opportunity to study all sides of an issue and to make their own decisions. Teachers should use discretion when selecting issues for study. Several criteria should be applied:

1. Are the children mature enough to thoroughly understand the issue?
2. Do the children have sufficient background experiences to critically appraise the issue?
3. Will the study of the issue help attain the goals of the school and community?
4. Is the issue of social, political, or economic significance?
5. Does the policy of the school permit the study of such an issue?
6. Will the children become better informed thoughtful citizens as a result of the study?

The manner in which a teacher approaches the study of controversial issues is of vital importance. The teacher who has a chip on his shoulder about the issue or one who is prejudiced, opinionated, or possesses an extreme point of view and teaches only one side of an issue would be wise to avoid the study. A teacher who feels he cannot discuss an issue without showing his prejudice does his children a disservice in attempting the study. One of the main purposes in having children research these issues is to develop in them the habit of approaching an issue with an open mind, securing the facts on all sides, and then making a decision if necessary. A prejudiced teacher who permits that prejudice to show defeats this purpose.

Approaches to the Study of Controversial Issues

The teacher must decide whether the issue will require an extensive study or can be handled in several class discussions with individual and group research. This decision will depend upon the children's expressed interest in the issue and the issue's relation to the previously stated criteria for their selection. The approach to a controversial issue requires extreme objectivity on the part of the teacher and the supplying of materials that present all sides of the issue.

Suppose a riot took place in your town last night. Today, depending upon the person reporting the event, it is being given labels such as "racial," "vandalism," "a demonstration against injustice," or "an overthrow of the laws." The children arrive in school very excited about the event and eager to discuss it. What do you do? How do you approach it? Obviously, you can't ignore the issue because it is a part of the children's world. Rather than permit the children to tell what they have heard about the riot, the teacher might suggest that they list a series of questions for which they will be required to secure answers.

1. How did the riot start?
2. Where did it start?
3. Is it known who was responsible for starting it?
4. How much damage was done?
5. Why did the riot begin?
6. Might it happen again?
7. What can be done to prevent it from happening again?

Answers to these questions should be found by listening to news reports (in school when possible) presented by several stations, reading papers, and talking to several people who were in the area, if this can be arranged. All children should record the answers they secure, give the source, and then compare them the next day when they arrive in school. If it is determined that the riot was caused by some deep-seated community problem, a thorough study of the issue should be undertaken by children in the intermediate grades if school policy permits. Young children should pursue the topic to the depth of their understanding and ability to secure information. Children should interview citizens of the community, assess their feelings about the problem, find out what laws govern the problem, and determine whether the laws are being enforced. The teacher should provide opportunity for children to discuss possible solutions to the problem. Children should learn that the true facts involved in this type of situation are often difficult to find. They should assess the validity of the information they secure.

Most controversial issues are so charged with emotion that it is difficult for the teacher to ask children to assess all sides of an issue unemotionally. A teacher may not always be successful in this task, but he should encourage his students to attempt to control their emotions and view issues objectively. Simple issues such as resolving the fair treatment of others in the classroom may be the starting point for understanding differences of opinion.

Any vitally alive social studies program must include the study of current affairs. If this study is omitted, the children are growing up outside the mainstream of society—the place where things are happening.

SELECTED REFERENCES

Chase, W. Linwood, *A Guide for the Elementary Social Studies Teacher.* Boston: Allyn & Bacon, Inc., 1966.

Crowder, William W., "Helping Elementary Children Understand Mass Persuasion Techniques," *Social Education,* XXXI (February, 1967), 119–21.

Howitt, Lillian C., *Enriching the Curriculum With Current Events.* New York: Teachers Practical Press, distributed by Atherton Press, 1964.

Jarolimek, John, *Social Studies in Elementary Education.* New York: The Macmillan Company, 1967.

Long, Harold M. and Robert N. King, *Improving the Teaching of World Affairs: The Glen Falls Story.* Washington, D.C.: National Council for the Social Studies, 1964.

Michaelis, John U., *Social Studies for Children in a Democracy* (4th ed.). Englewood Cliffs, N.J.: Prentice-Hall, Inc., 1968.

Sheridan, Jack, "Thursday Is Current Events Day," *Social Education,* XXXII (May, 1968), 461.

CHAPTER EIGHT

International Understandings

SHOULD CHILDREN LEARN ABOUT THEIR CULTURE AND THE sub-cultures in their own country before they learn about cultures around the world? Does an understanding of a culture quite removed from the children help them understand the differences among peoples in their own environment? Jerome Bruner contends that the contrast of studying a culture that is removed enhances the meaningfulness of the here and now. He suggests that without the contrast, the familiar is apt to be shallow.[1]

Preston, however, suggests that depth studies of familiar institutions should be conducted first to help children develop an awareness of the significant relationships. Understanding the significant relationships of their own institutions permits children to successfully contrast these with those

---

[1]Jerome S. Bruner, *Toward A Theory of Instruction* (Cambridge: The Belknap Press of Harvard University Press, 1966), p. 92.

found in other cultures.[2] Either theory promotes the need for the study of other cultures.

Why should children learn of other cultures? One of the primary reasons for teaching international understandings is to promote knowledge of the delicate balance of the relationships among the countries of the world today. The nations controlling most of the nuclear weapons today—the United States, the Soviet Union, and China—wield considerable power individually and collectively, and their lack of agreement on basic ideological principles is of vital importance. In addition, the developing nations of the world resent their power. The developing nations exhibit a natural quest for recognition as they attempt to assert their new found growth. The development of an understanding of the culture of these nations, their motivation, and the problems they face is essential to the survival of our nation.

Christensen relates some interesting facts about what he calls the technologically less advanced nations, the nations where two-thirds of the people of the world live.

1. Even when the vast Soviet area of Siberia is excluded, over half of the human family lives in Asia.
2. Most of the world's people are non-white.
3. Most of the world's people are non-Christian.
4. Most people live in rapid population growth areas and are members of large families.
5. Most of the world's people make their precarious living as farmers and craftsmen and depend heavily on hand and animal labor.
6. Most of the world's people are poor in terms of money income.
7. Most of the world's people are very poorly fed.
8. Most of the world's people are sick and in need of medical care.
9. Despite the high priority that school development programs now receive in the technologically less-advanced nations, the fact remains that about one adult in three in the world is illiterate.
10. Countries in which most people live depend very little on trade and many depend on only a few specialized exports.
11. Most of the world's people live under new and relatively inexperienced and, in many cases, unstable governments.
12. The technologically less advanced nations are involved in the "Revolution of Rising Expectations" as they attempt to imitate the more advanced nations in technological development.[3]

2Ralph C. Preston, "Familiarity and Contrast as Curriculum Principles," *Social Education*, XXXI (October, 1967), 493.
3David E. Christensen, "Two-Thirds of the World," *Social Education*, XXXI (March, 1967), 212–17.

To present a complete view of the world, Christensen continues with ten facts about the other one-third of the world, the technologically advanced nations.

1. Most of the people in TA nations are white, Christian, and live in the mid-latitude areas of North America, Europe, and the Soviet Union.
2. Most of the people in the TA nations live in rapidly growing towns and cities.
3. Most people in TA countries live at levels of nutrition and health that are far above minimum standards, and average longevity is half again as large as it is in the less developed countries.
4. Most people in the TA countries have incomes that are large enough to provide much more than a bare minimum level of living.
5. The economics of TA countries are completely commercialized and depend on high rates of production and consumption of all kinds of goods and services.
6. People and nations in all technologically advanced areas exist at a high level of interdependence and economic vulnerability.
7. Technologically advanced countries are governed by experienced, mature governments that are elected by and generally responsive to an informed electorate.
8. Literacy rates are high in TA countries and, in general, people are somewhat more informed than in less-advanced countries about conditions and problems in their own country and elsewhere in the world.
9. The very success of the TA countries—in their research and development programs, in their accumulation of wealth, and in many other ways—has brought on the most difficult and change-fraught problem that these areas ever have had to face: automation and the cybernation revolution.
10. People in many of the TA nations view their advantaged situation with a feeling of uneasiness about the power of science and the inability of national governments to provide security despite large military expenditures.[4]

Obviously, these revealing facts underline the necessity for including the study of cultures that are non-white, non-Christian, and non-Western. Our nation, as one of the technologically advanced nations, must educate the next generation of citizens to cope with the problems of the technologically less advanced nations, in which two-thirds of the world's people now live.

Frequently cited by authorities as a sickness of our nation is the growing lack of concern for others displayed by our citizens. Soul searching for the cause of this sickness turns one's attention to the school; however,

---

[4]David E. Christensen, "One-Third of the World," *Social Education*, XXXI (April, 1967), 294–98.

the school certainly should not be the only institution to assess its responsibility for this apparent sickness. We might ask the question "Have we failed to develop sensitivity and concern for other peoples?" If Bruner's belief that familiarity does not necessarily promote understanding is true, it may be best to help children develop empathy for peoples of other cultures and their problems. Children can then transfer and relate this empathy to their own culture.

The mobility of people today definitely affects our lives. Many communities are made up of peoples from all over the world. These peoples bring their traditions and customs with them, and children need to understand these differences in cultures. Children should have an understanding of the effects the environment and history of a country have upon its culture.

The interdependence of nations is another understanding that should be developed with children. Our technologically advanced nation relies heavily on other countries for "raw materials, some foods, petroleum, and other goods to maintain the higher level of living . . ."[5] Equally important are the markets provided by other countries for our manufactured goods. Good relationships must be maintained with these countries to enable a continuation of the exchange of products.

Our lives are affected daily, whether we are aware of it or not, by the actions of people all over the world. A nation cannot remain isolated and unaffected by these actions; consequently, children must acquire some knowledge of other cultures if they are to participate in the affairs of the world.

The objectives developed for the promotion of international understandings are summarized as follows:

To increase understanding of one's own culture.

To facilitate understanding of the relationships among the powerful and less advanced countries of the world.

To increase sensitivity and concern for others.

To promote an understanding of the interdependence of peoples.

To develop a more thorough understanding of the effect on our nation of the actions of people around the world.

Guidelines for Selecting Cultures for Study

Because it is obviously impossible to study all cultures, it is important that the teacher select topics for study wisely. He should select the

[5]Christensen, "One-Third of the World," p. 297.

cultures that are most important for his group of children. Cultures that relate most closely with the lives of the children should be introduced first. Countries represented by the backgrounds of the children in the classroom are good examples. If a child has moved to this country from Japan, he brings a rich background of experiences that he can share with the other children. Also, this child will feel more a part of the group when the other children become involved in a study of his birthplace. Parents of these children are often willing to share their knowledge and realia of the country. If no children in the classroom have lived in another land, ancestral countries might be studied. The study of a country to be visited by any of the children would also be appropriate. A country that is spotlighted in the news as a trouble spot, disaster area, or location of an interesting event also provides a good choice for study. Examples of such countries are Vietnam during the war, Turkey after an earthquake, and Mexico at the time of the Olympics.

Neighboring countries of Canada and Mexico should be included for study to develop an understanding of how countries maintain friendly relationships. Children should realize that we have long unprotected borders between these countries, and they should be aware of the cooperative ventures we've undertaken such as the St. Lawrence Seaway. More of the children might have an opportunity to visit these countries.

Cultures that are quite similar to our own as well as those that provide contrasts should be studied. Select one culture of each type to be included after the study of some aspect of our culture. These studies enable children to comprehend the reasons why cultures develop as they do.

When to Start

Early exposure to other cultures through personal associations and the mass media suggest that kindergarten is not too soon to begin teaching children knowledge about other cultures that is within their understanding. The Anthropology Project at the University of Georgia and the Greater Cleveland Social Science Program provide learning experiences about other cultures at beginning levels. The Georgia Project adheres to the philosophy of Bruner and selects a culture, the Arunta, that is relatively unknown to pupils and teacher. The philosophy underlying this selection is that neither teacher nor pupils will approach the study of the culture with any preconceived ideas about it.

The Greater Cleveland Program includes in kindergarten: Children in Other Lands: Globe Study, Japan, Mexico, American Samoa, Lapland, Nigeria, Central Congo, and England.

The study of selected cultures throughout the elementary grades is extremely important. The method used for the study can be based on problem solving, unit development, or a combination of these approaches. A depth study of one culture—especially at the intermediate-grade level —is preferable to cursory studies of several cultures, which fail to develop any real understandings.

No one would deny that a thorough understanding of the United States, its institutions, heritage, and democratic procedures is important and vital to any social studies program. However, the exclusive study of our nation without learning about other cultures is unwise in our present world.

ATMOSPHERE OF THE CLASSROOM

The attitude of the teacher and the atmosphere that is established in the classroom are vital to the development of international understandings. A teacher who displays anything but complete acceptance of every child in the class regardless of differences in race, religion, or national origin would most probably fail in an attempt to teach the children to be accepting of others. Even the casual comments a teacher makes about children in the classroom or about individuals of another culture have an effect upon children. It is difficult to hide real feelings behind a facade, for children soon detect falseness and a lack of sincerity in a person.

A classroom where there is an attitude of mutual respect for and sensitivity to the feelings of others provides the proper atmosphere for developing empathy for peoples of different cultures. Such an attitude does not just happen—activities should be planned to aid its growth. Children have a natural tendency to be concerned about themselves and their own problems. They need to discover the pleasure that comes from assisting others. A classroom partner plan for helping with one another's work, committee assignments, assisting in the school library, and working in the safety patrol are examples of activities within the school that help children develop the ability to empathize with others. Projects initiated in the community such as cleaning up a local lot for a playground, collecting toys for underprivileged children, singing or performing at the home for the elderly, and participating in fund-raising drives for worthy causes are identified as representative of the type of activity needed. It is doubtful that children will be able to develop empathy for people of another culture with whom they have no contact if they have little feeling for those with whom they associate almost daily.

Involvement with people of another culture:

Actively participating, when possible, with people of another culture is certainly more worthwhile than merely reading about them in a book or seeing a film. Activities that provide participation are:

1. Pen pals—Children acquire names of those in another land who wish to correspond with someone.
2. Exchange programs—Classes exchange samples of art work, scrapbooks, etc. with classes in another country. (Write: Art For World Friendship, Friendly Acres, Media, Pennsylvania.)
3. UNICEF—At Halloween, children trick or treat for money for the children's fund of the United Nations.
4. CARE—Money earned by class projects such as bake sales, movies, candy sales, and car washes can be donated to aid people in the country of your choice. CARE buys food and tools to help the people.
5. Visitors—Visitors from another culture are invited to the school for discussions of their country, demonstration of their language, and display of any realia they may have brought with them. The contact with an actual resident of another culture makes the culture appear more realistic to the children.
6. Adopting Children—There are several plans that permit financial assistance to children in countries where special help is needed. An example is the Christian Children's Fund, Box 511, Richmond, Virginia 23204. The agencies send a picture of the child with his background information and permit the exchange of letters.

ACTIVITIES FOR PRIMARY GRADES

The young child is especially interested in learning about the aspects within another culture that are most important to him in his own daily activities. Questions he wants answered are:

1. What games do they play?
2. What is their school like?
3. What type of clothes do they wear?
4. What are their favorite foods?
5. Do they have toys?
6. What type of work does the father do?
7. What are the houses like?
8. How can I travel to the country, and how long will it take?

Learning experiences that develop from these questions are numerous. Map and globe skills can be acquired by determining the country's location. A trip planned from the child's home to the other country aids in developing space relationships; and in planning the time required for the trip, the child acquires more knowledge of distances. Children can play games from the country and learn its simple folk dances. Singing the songs and listening to the music from a country also adds to the flavor of the study.

Children's books are excellent sources for children of any age, but they are especially helpful with young children. Generally, these books contain stories of children from other countries, and they describe their customs and cultures in terms that children can easily understand. It is important to be certain that the information in the book is accurate. Care in the selection of books should prevent the use of those that present only the differences in culture and fail to show the similarities of all children no matter where they live. It is interesting to compare the folk tales, fables, and myths of other lands with those of our own country.

A comparison study of the holidays and festivals around the world or in individual countries aids understanding. A country's religious celebrations, in particular, reveal considerable information about the historical background of the country. Preparing food from different lands, discussing meals served in the school or home that originated in other countries, and visiting zoos to identify animals from other lands are additional activities that can be planned.

These activities should not be presented to children as a haphazard collection of things to do; rather, they should be regarded as the type of learning experiences that can be planned when studying another culture. The teacher may emphasize pertinent activities when working with a particular culture. Different aspects would be emphasized for different studies, of course.

ACTIVITIES FOR INTERMEDIATE GRADES

The maturity level of the intermediate-grade child permits depth study of the cultures. These children should learn about the historical and geographical factors that influence a country's culture. The social, political, and economic problems of the cultures under study should be investigated, for most intermediate-grade children can understand the situation and propose solutions.

Many of the activities discussed for primary grades can also be used in the intermediate grades; however, the older children's questions will be more penetrating, for example:

1. How are the people governed?
2. What are the important industries?

3. What are the agricultural products?
4. Who are some of the famous people of the country?
5. What freedoms do the people possess?
6. How did the country develop?
7. What are the people like?
8. What position does the country play in the world?

These questions require depth study, and intermediate children are capable of more extensive research to obtain answers.

Children should learn of the activities of the United States government in its aid to other nations. Programs such as the Marshall Plan and AID have invested vast amounts of money for development projects in nations. Critics of these projects who portray the ugly American image should also be discussed, for some of the projects have failed to meet expectations. However, children should be aware of the many people who have benefited from them.

A thorough study of the United Nations should be initiated in the intermediate grades. It is important that children gain an understanding of its role in maintaining good international relationships. The responsibilities of each organ of the United Nations are important factors to stress. Countries that have major responsibilities at the time of the study such as the countries of the president of the United Nations and chairman of the Security Council may be investigated in greater depth.

In developing international understandings, it is significant to remember that this learning must be an on-going process, not a once-a-year activity. Every opportunity to relate daily activities with world-mindedness should be used to advantage.[6]

SELECTED REFERENCES

Around the Corner: Preparing Today's Students for Tomorrow's World, Pub. No. 8081. Washington, D.C.: U.S. Department of State, 1966.

Chase, Judith W., *Books to Build World Friendship*. Dobbs Ferry, New York: Oceana Publications, Inc., 1964.

International Communications Foundation, 9033 Wilshire Blvd., Beverly Hills, California.

"International Understanding in an Era of Nationalism, Paul Hanna interviews Arnold Toynbee," *Phi Delta Kappan*, XLVI (December, 1967), 170–77.

[6]Harold M. Long and Robert N. King, *Improving the Teaching of World Affairs: The Glen Falls Story* (Washington, D.C.: National Council for the Social Studies, 1964).

Joyce, Bruce R., "The World Widened Elementary School," *Elementary School Journal*, LXII (April, 1962), 343–45.

Kenworthy, Leonard S., *Free and Inexpensive Materials on World Affairs*. New York: Teachers College, 1963.

Kenworthy, Leonard S., "The International Dimension of Elementary Schools," *Phi Delta Kappan*, XLVI (December, 1967), 203–7.

Mehlinger, Howard and James M. Becker, *International Dimensions in the Social Studies*, 38th Yearbook. Washington, D.C.: National Council for the Social Studies, 1968.

Teaching About the United Nations. Washington, D.C.: U.S. Office of Education, 1964.

Can skills developed in the social studies be used in other subject areas?

Skill Development

Opportunities for skill development in the social studies are numerous. In addition to the specific skills needed in the social studies, the subject provides a real purpose for use of the skills introduced in other curriculum areas such as language arts, science, mathematics, art, music, and physical education. The 33rd Yearbook of the National Council for the Social Studies analyzes skills of shared responsibility and those pertaining specifically to the social studies.

I. Skills that are a definite but shared responsibility of the social studies.

1. Locating information.
2. Organizing information.
3. Evaluating information.
4. Acquiring information through reading.
5. Acquiring information through listening and observing.

6. Communicating orally and in writing.
7. Interpreting pictures, charts, graphs, tables.
8. Working with others.

II. Skills that are a major responsibility of the social studies.

1. Reading social studies materials.
2. Applying problem-solving and critical-thinking skills to social issues.
3. Interpreting maps and globes.
4. Understanding time and chronology.[1]

The Council suggests that development should be based on the following principles of learning and teaching:

1. The skill should be taught functionally, in the concept of a topic of study, rather than a separate exercise.
2. The learner must understand the meaning and purpose of the skill, and have motivation for developing it.
3. The learner should be carefully supervised in his first attempts to apply the skill, so that he will form correct habits from the beginning.
4. The learner needs repeated opportunities to practice the skill, with immediate evaluation so that he knows where he has succeeded or failed in his performance.
5. The learner needs individual help, through diagnostic measures and follow-up exercises, since not all members of any group learn at exactly the same rate or retain equal amounts of what they have learned.
6. Skill instruction should be presented at increasing levels of difficulty, moving from the simple to the more complex; the resulting growth in skills should be cumulative as the learner moves through school, with each level of instruction building on and reinforcing what has been taught previously.
7. Students should be helped, at each stage, to generalize the skills, by applying them in many and varied situations, in this way maximum transfer of learning can be achieved.
8. The program of instruction should be sufficiently flexible to allow skills to be taught as they are needed by the learner; many skills should be developed concurrently.[2]

Part four (1) discusses committee work as the primary vehicle for developing intellectual, expressive, and social skills in social studies and (2) presents map and globe skills with suggested activities.

[1]Helen McCracken Carpenter, ed., *Skill Development in Social Studies*, 33rd Yearbook (Washington, D.C.: National Council for the Social Studies, 1963), pp. 310–11.
[2]Carpenter, ed., *Skill Development in Social Studies*, pp. 311–12.

Committee work was selected because of the many opportunities for skill development it offers. Committee work in social studies is a representative activity that is effective in developing skills; these skills can, of course, be developed in other ways.

Because map and globe skills are of a particularly specialized nature and are frequently neglected by the teacher, they are given special emphasis.

CHAPTER NINE

Working in Committees

EXPERIENCE IN WORKING IN COMMITTEES FOR THE ATTAINMENT of specific goals develops skill in cooperative behavior. The ability to get along with others is a skill that should be acquired as early as possible. As he enters school, the young child is often self-centered and frequently unwilling to share materials with others. He learns the skills of cooperative behavior by sharing playthings; working on projects with other children; and participating in group activities such as singing, dancing, and listening to stories. At the kindergarten level, committees should be small consisting of two or three children; and the task should be of a simple nature. Building a house with blocks, getting the milk, or cleaning up materials in the play areas are suggested as beginning activities for committee work. Later in kindergarten and in first grade, more formal tasks can be assigned such as preparing a story for creative dramatics, drawing a movie roll of a story, or finding answers to questions by looking at pictures. One first-grade class organized a pet show with committees of children responsible for invitations, judging, refreshments, prizes, and care of pets. Children soon learn that the success of such an activity is dependent upon each person cooperating and completing his share of the task.

Continual involvement in committee work throughout the elementary grades is necessary to maintain and refine skill in working together. As children mature, they are capable of working in larger groups (of perhaps five or six members) and of completing more difficult tasks. It is crucial that the teacher establish a definite purpose for committee work and that the children understand this purpose.

ORGANIZATION

The method of selecting members for committees can vary depending upon the group of children and the purpose. Classes of children who have few discipline problems and get along well with one another can generally be permitted to select committee memberships of their choice, based on each individual's interest in a particular subject or task. However, classes of children who experience considerable difficulty in getting along, have discipline problems, or have too many leaders should be organized in committees by the teacher. At times, it is beneficial for the teacher to select particular students for a committee in order to meet individual differences. For example, the child who is exceptional in art may be placed on a committee in which he can use his talent. Or, the child not very adept in research skills should receive help when placed on a committee of children more capable. It is not necessarily good, however, to place outstanding children with the very slow, for too great a discrepancy in ability may result in frustration for all concerned.

The teacher who has never worked with committees before or a class that has not had experience in working in committees may wish to begin the activity one committee at a time. Using this method, the teacher organizes one committee to work on a task; and at the completion of its responsibility, she organizes another committee. This method allows the teacher more time to work with each group to guide its activities. After all members of the class have participated in this experience, the whole class can be organized into committees.

TEACHER-PUPIL PLANNING

Successful committee experiences depend considerably upon the routines established within the classroom. Children respond more favorably when they have the opportunity to aid in developing the guidelines for a project. The following is an example of the dialogue of a class planning for committee work. The children are fourth graders who have had previous, but limited, experience working in committees.

TEACHER. What is the first thing a committee should do after the members have been selected?

GEORGE. We should decide on someone to be a chairman.

TEACHER. How do you make this decision?

JANE. We can hold an election nominating people and voting on them.

BILL. Yes, but that takes too long. You can have each person decide who he wants and write the name on a slip of paper.

TEACHER. What type of person makes the best chairman?

SALLY. Someone who isn't too bossy and always telling you what to do.

SAM. Someone who will do his share, but also help you if you need it.

TEACHER. Suppose we list the responsibiliites of a chairman.

The children's completed list of responsibilities for the chairman follows:

The chairman should:

1. Understand the responsibility of his committee.
2. Help each person understand his task.
3. Be sure each person completes his task.
4. Be accepting of the opinions and suggestions of committee members.
5. Report the committee's progress and problems concerning materials to the class.
6. Be sure members share materials.

TEACHER. What responsibilities do the members of the committee have?

JIM. We need to be sure that we do our share of the work and not wait to be told.

MISSY. Don't forget that sharing materials is a committee member's responsibility too.

The completed list was placed on a chart for all to observe when needed. These are the points listed:

Committee members should:

1. Share materials with others.
2. Listen to the committee members' and the chairman's suggestions.
3. Complete your task on time.

4. Do your share of the work.
5. Be willing to help others.

TEACHER. Are there certain things we should all remember when working in committees?
MARY. Work quietly, so you won't disturb others.
RICK. Clean up your materials at the end of the period.
BILL. I think that the big thing is to get your work done on time so others won't have to wait for you.
SHELLY. Also, stick to your topic and don't spoil someone else's report.

The type of responses listed here are typical of those most classes will offer. The crucial aspect is not the content of the response but rather the process involved, whereby the children take an active part in the decision-making process, which affects their behavior as they work in committees. With young children, a teacher may find it necessary to be more directive in her questioning. For example, the teacher might ask questions such as: When we play a game and choose a leader, how do we do this? What is the leader's job?

The guidelines that have been established by the class should be referred to daily before beginning the work. In addition, when a problem arises, the teacher should suggest that the children analyze the cause of the problem and check the guidelines for a solution. Children become more self-reliant and self-disciplined when they share in the process of making the rules.

Intellectual Skills

Within the framework of committee responsibility, intellectual skills of using reference materials, locating information, outlining and note-taking, critical thinking, and making oral and written reports are utilized. Each of these skills will be discussed in detail. Quickly recognized is the ease with which the social studies and the language arts can be interrelated through the development of these skills.

USING REFERENCE MATERIALS

As children search for information pertaining to their assigned topic, they will need assistance in using a variety of resource materials.

1. Library—In preparing to use the library for committee assignments, the children should learn the arrangement of the card catalog, the placement of books on the shelves, and the procedure for checking out books. The topic under study may be used as an example to be located in the card catalog, etc.

2. Encyclopedia—One of young children's favorite sources of information is the encyclopedia, because its organization makes it easy for them to locate topics. Frequently, children copy information from this book without any understanding. The vocabulary may be too difficult, and the children do not look up the words in the dictionary. Guidelines should be established for using the encyclopedia.

   The child should ask himself these questions:
   a. Do I understand the information given about the topic?
   b. Are there any vocabulary words I do not know?
   c. How can I best report this information to the class?
   d. Will an outline of the information be enough or should I take notes?
   e. Are there cross-references where I might secure additional information about the topic?
   f. If I prepare a written report, can I complete it in my own words?

3. Textbook—The textbook can be used for background reading by the entire class prior to committee research, or individual committees can use the text to secure information about their aspect of the topic. The teacher should be sure that the children understand the organization of the text and that the reading level is suitable. When available, a variety of texts or multi-texts provide the opportunity to compare viewpoints and information presented by different authors.

4. Primary sources—Work with primary source material (original source of information without some other person's interpretation) is valuable in helping children draw their own conclusions, interpret the facts presented, and evaluate the validity of the material. G. P. Putnam and Sons have produced "Jackdaws," which are kits of primary source material. Each kit is organized around a topic such as "Columbus and the Discovery of America." They include reproductions of actual documents from this early historical period.

   Another primary source of information is obtained by conducting interviews and surveys. Children should prepare their questions for the interview in advance. An example of an interview the children might conduct would be questioning an official about the building of a recreational park for the city:
   a. Where will the park be located?
   b. What type of equipment will it include?
   c. How much will it cost the taxpayers?
   d. When will it be completed?
   e. Why is it being built?

After securing information from a primary source, the child should compare it, if possible, with its coverage in the newspaper. The children should try to answer these questions: Does the paper report the same information? Does it express a bias? If so, why? Is it possible that the reporters were given incorrect information?

5. Other sources—Newspapers, magazines, films, filmstrips, and recordings are sources children can use to secure information. They need to evaluate the sources to determine which are most valid.

LOCATING INFORMATION

Skills children need for locating information are: (1) knowledge of available resources, as discussed in the preceding section; (2) understanding of how the resource is organized—alphabetically, topically, etc.; (3) ability to use the table of contents, which lists the major headings; (4) ability to use the index, which cites a page number for each entry; (5) knowledge of cross references, which indicate a related topic that may give additional information; (6) ability to glean information from illustrations; and (7) ability to read maps, graphs, and charts.

OUTLINING AND NOTETAKING

Information is outlined to provide a skeleton of the important points. An outline is useful in helping a child organize his information; however, useless outlining of page after page of material for practice is a waste of time. Because an outline presents information in a shortened and simplified form giving only the important points about a topic, children should start with the short form. The main points about a topic are called the main topics or main headings and are designated by Roman numerals. Points about the topic that fall under the main headings are subtopics or subheadings and are designated by capital letters. Details about the subtopics follow them and are designated by numbers, as in the following example:

I. Africa
   A. Geography
      1. Mountains
      2. Rainforests
      3. Rivers

Notetaking necessitates a decision regarding the purpose of the information. Before they start to take notes, children should be encouraged to ask themselves, (1) Am I attempting to entertain someone with the information? (2) Am I selecting information that I think an audience would not know? and (3) Am I selecting information I think everyone should know about the topic? After they have answered these questions, they can begin to select the appropriate information.

CRITICAL THINKING

Children are encouraged to use a variety of resource materials as they search for information to fulfill their committee tasks. The resource materials should stimulate critical thinking, initiating questions such as: Does the author of the material express a point of view? Does he use any methods of propaganda in his writing? Does the information vary from source to source? Is the author stating fact or opinion?

When the information has been collected and reported to the class, another opportunity for developing thinking skills arises. Analysis of this information is necessary. Did the committee look at all sides of the issue? Did they present the information accurately or did they express their own opinions? The teacher is responsible for directing these questions to the children so that each child will become accustomed to asking them of himself.

ORAL AND WRITTEN REPORTS

Skills needed for oral and written reports can be developed in the wide variety of activities involved in presenting committee reports to the class. These skills can also be identified as expressive skills, for the children express themselves in writing, speaking, or drawing. After research has been completed, the development of a method of sharing each committee's information with the group becomes necessary. Criteria for the success of this method are: (1) Did the children gain knowledge from the reports? (2) Did they exhibit an interest in the reports. The guidelines established for reporting include:

1. Present the information in such a way that others will be interested in the topic.
2. Be sure the information is accurate and easily understood. Don't obscure the information in gimmicks to develop interest.

The type of information that has been secured will, to a certain extent, determine the choice of presentation. Children should learn what type of presentation best communicates the information they have to report. The oral skills to be developed are:

1. To acquire poise and confidence in a group situation.
2. To speak with expression.
3. To acquire fluency in phrasing.
4. To speak clearly and slowly.
5. To express an idea so that it may be understood.
6. To adjust volume of voice to size of group.

PANEL DISCUSSIONS

Organizing information for a panel discussion is generally better accomplished by intermediate-grade children, but variations of the panel
can be presented by young children. For example, first- or second-grade
committee members can prepare their part of the presentation on charts,
with or without pictures they have drawn. If a child has difficulty with
writing, the teacher can prepare a chart from the child's dictation or
the child can use pictures and give information in his own words. Questions asked back and forth by the panel members are beneficial if they
are prepared before the discussion so children know what to expect.

Intermediate-grade children need to be cautioned against merely reading their reported information rather than discussing it. A time limit of
two to three minutes for each discussant requires the children to be
concise and to select the most pertinent information. To increase interest
in their discussion, children can use visual aids such as illustrations,
transparencies, charts, graphs, or a short filmstrip. Points children should
remember for any oral presentation are:

1. Stick to the topic of your report.
2. Speak clearly and slowly enough to be heard by all.
3. Use inflections in your voice.
4. Maintain good eye contact with your audience.

DEBATES

Debate, to be effective, should be used by intermediate-grade children.
They are more capable of the extensive research needed to dig out the
pros and cons of an issue. The issue selected for the debate should be one
that provokes critical analysis and presents the possibility for taking a
position. An example might be—Resolved: The United States Government should spend sufficient funds for research to attempt to send a man
to the moon or, Resolved: The voting age in the United States should
be lowered to eighteen. Rules should be established for the debate, with
time limits set for each presentation and rebuttal. The children should

be cautioned about becoming too emotional over the debate. They should understand that a debate is won by presenting the most persuasive argument for their side.

ROLE-PLAYING

A historical incident or an attempted solution to a problem can be role-played by a committee. In this activity, the children can use their own language and ideas, based on their research, to depict some incident. Role-playing the signing of the Declaration of Independence or peace treaty talks will help children understand and remember these events. Role-playing gives children the opportunity to express emotions and to attempt to involve themselves in a situation. Children at any grade level can participate in this activity.

TV OR RADIO PROGRAMS

Patterning an oral report after the format of a TV or radio program adds an element of interest. Some children may even add the commercials to make it realistic. Children who have difficulty with oral presentations are often less self-conscious when given the opportunity to pretend to be someone else or to hide behind a microphone.

Show formats such as "This Is Your Life" or "You Were There" are appropriate for historical incidents, while an interview type format like the "Today Show" is good for factual and opinion reports. The "Huntley-Brinkley" news format is enjoyed by children for factual reporting.

DRAMATIC PRESENTATIONS

Similar to role-playing, but with more definite lines and usually costumes and props, skits and plays can be used by children to present their committee reports. Once again this activity increases the element of interest, and children can hide their self-consciousness behind a character in the play. An example of this type of activity might be a skit depicting a day in the life of a child in Mexico, showing his food, clothing, home, and customs. This information is much more easily remembered through visual representation.

The lines for a dramatic presentation can be taped. Children can practice by taping and playing back the presentation until they are satisfied with the performance. Preparation of any oral report can be improved by use of the tape recorder. Each child has the opportunity to hear his mistakes and improve the quality of his voice.

Written Reports

Skills to be developed in the written reports are:

1. Organize the information in a meaningful sequence.
2. Select the relevant information.
3. Use correct language, capitalization, and punctuation.

The information gathered by a committee can be compiled in a written report when the teacher notes a need for increased skill in this area. The written report might be assembled in a scrapbook with illustrations or in a booklet form. Children can use a textbook format with a table of contents, chapter headings, glossary, etc. All members of the committee should agree on the same format. Reports such as these should be interesting, concise, written in the child's language, and available for all to read. A display of the reports can remain on the reading table until all have had the chance to read them. These reports can also be used for reference when possible.

Graphic Reports

Committees can present their research information through graphic representations. For example, the preparation of a wall mural depicting methods of transportation may be more easily interpreted by children than verbal description. Or the building of a model village may relate more to children about life in Peru than a dozen written reports. The child who is more adept at painting than writing or speaking can meet with success in this type of activity.

Social Skills

Social skills, which are so necessary in our society, are developed through most learning experiences in school; however, committee membership provides many fine opportunities for their practice. Learning to get along with others, sharing materials, the give and take of opinions, and assuming responsibility are important skills to be acquired if the committees are to be successful. If these skills are acquired during committee work, the results should carry over into activities in other areas such as on the playground, during other class work, and after school in the neighborhood.

The organization of a committee necessitates getting along with others. Each member must be willing to accept the guidance of the chairman. The membership of a committee may not consist of each person's best friends; therefore, the child must learn to cooperate with any classmate. If committee tasks are to be completed, members must be willing to share materials and readily respect the opinions of others. Each committee member has a responsibility that he must assume if success is to be achieved.

Frequently, classes that have failed to develop any real group feeling or "esprit de corp" will be more successful after the experience of working together in committees.

SELECTED REFERENCES

Bergeson, Clarence O., "Using Learning Resources in Social Studies Skill Development," *Social Education*, XXXI (March, 1967), 227.

Carpenter, Helen McCracken, "The Role of Skills in Elementary Social Studies," *Social Education*, XXXI (March, 1967), 219.

Carpenter, Helen McCracken, ed., *Skill Development in Social Studies*, 33rd Yearbook. Washington, D.C.: National Council for the Social Studies, 1963.

Davis, O. L., Jr., "Building Skills for Social Study in the Middle Grades," *Social Education*, XXXI (March, 1967), 224.

Douglas, Malcolm P., *Social Studies From Theory to Practice in Elementary Education*. Philadelphia: J. B. Lippincott Co., 1967.

Dunfee, Maxine and Helen Sagl, *Social Studies Through Problem Solving*. New York: Holt, Rinehart & Winston, Inc., 1966.

Foster, Clifford D., "Skills in the Elementary School Social Studies Curriculum," *Social Education*, XXXI (March, 1967), 230.

Groeschell, Robert, "Curriculum Provisions for Individual Differences," *Social Education*, XXXI (May, 1967), 416.

Jarolimek, John, "Skills Teaching in the Primary Grades," *Social Education*, XXXI (March, 1967), 222.

O'Connor, John R., "Reading Skills in the Social Studies," *Social Education*, XXXI (February, 1967), 104.

Rogers, Vincent R., "The Individual and the Social Studies," *Social Education,* XXXI (May, 1967), 405.

Shaftel, Fannie R. and George Shaftel, *Role-Playing for Social Values: Decision Making in the Social Studies.* Englewood Cliffs, N.J.: Prentice-Hall, Inc., 1967.

Skeel, Dorothy J., *Developing Creative Ability.* South Holland, Ill.: H. Wilson Corp., 1967.

Skeel, Dorothy J., *Developing Language Arts Skills.* South Holland Ill.: H. Wilson Corp., 1968.

Smith, James A., *Creative Teaching of the Social Studies.* Boston: Allyn & Bacon, Inc., 1967.

CHAPTER TEN

Map and Globe Skills

"WHERE DO YOU LIVE?" "WHAT IS IT NEAR?" "HOW CAN I GET there?" These are common questions asked by a person attempting to locate someone's home. Depending upon the location and the individual's ability in locational skills, he might answer by naming the place, expressing the distance from his present location to his home, expressing this distance in terms of the time required to go there, or he might designate the location by readings of latitude and longitude to be more exact. With the increased speed of today's travel, the time involved in reaching one's destination has changed; however, the skills required to locate a place remain the same. Mass media, which includes a great number of unfamiliar places in its reporting, and the increased mobility of people enhance the study of locational skills. Map reading requires the learning of a new language, which enables the individual to interpret map symbols. Six **basic** skills have been recognized as comprehensive for map reading and interpretation:

149

1. Ability to orient the map and note directions.
2. Ability to recognize the scale of a map and compute distances.
3. Ability to locate places on maps and globes by means of grid systems.
4. Ability to express relative locations.
5. Ability to read map symbols.
6. Ability to compare maps and to make inferences.[1]

Limited research has been completed to determine children's ability with map skills at varying grade levels. On the basis of child development studies, Bacon contends that young children learn to think geographically much sooner than they learn to think historically.[2] Rushdoony found that primary children were able to profit from instruction in map-reading skills recommended for fourth and fifth graders. He suggests that curriculums be revised to introduce map skills to children at an earlier level. He also found high positive correlation between map-reading achievement and intelligence, reading achievement, and arithmetic achievement.[3]

Most social studies educators agree that effective instruction in map and globe skills is accomplished through developmental tasks and that this instruction should be conducted in the context of the study of a topic. Thus, the six basic skills will be developed in the primary and intermediate grades in the context of a suggested topic. In the following discussion of methods for teaching map skills, the six basic skills (listed above) will be indicated by the number to which they correspond in the list. In mastering these map skills, children will need to build upon a progression of learning experiences These suggested activities are representative and are not intended to be the only ones developed at each grade level.

KINDERGARTEN

As the children study the family and home, they develop a map of the community, using blocks placed on butcher paper to represent the school and their homes (5). A trip outside the school on a sunny day enables the children to note the location of the sun when they arrive at school and when they leave. With this knowledge, the children are able to place

---

[1] *Skill Development in Social Studies*, 33rd Yearbook (Washington D.C.: National Council for the Social Studies, 1963), p. 157.

[2] *New Viewpoints in Geography*, 29th Yearbook (Washington D.C.: National Council for the Social Studies, 1959), p. 150.

[3] Haig A. Rushdoony, "Achievement in Map-Reading: An Experimental Study," *The Elementary School Journal*, LXIV (November, 1963), 74.

the sun on their map as a directional guide (1). The children place blocks on the map to locate the other outstanding buildings such as the fire station, library, and churches relative to their homes (4). Beginning at the school, they count the number of blocks (in a city) or miles (in a rural area) to their homes (2). The teacher draws the same map on a piece of paper representing their homes and other buildings with drawings (5). The children compare their block map with the teacher's map to locate their homes (6). The simple slate or physical-relief globe is then used to locate the placement of their homes in relation to the other areas of the world (3, 1, 5).

FIRST GRADE

Young children are fascinated by the study of a culture different from their own, especially one they think is quite far away. Japan is an example of a culture that might be used in first grade. The children first locate Japan on a simple globe and realize that it is a group of islands (1, 5). The teacher uses a tub of water and a cardboard representation of the islands to help develop this concept (6). The children note the direction of Japan from their homes (1). In an attempt to determine the distance of Japan from the children's homes, compute the time in days it would take to reach the islands by plane or boat (2). Use a floor map of the world with land masses and water indicated, place a toy plane and boat on the map, and move them at their approximate speed of travel —one day of school for the plane and five days of school for the boat (1, 2, 3, 4, 5). Use a globe that has an attachment showing the division of day and night to interpret the time differences (6, 5).

SECOND GRADE

Wall maps can be introduced at this level, but transition from the floor map to the wall map should be provided. During a study of community helpers, children can make a large floor map using symbols to locate the buildings of the helpers such as the fire station and police station (1, 4, 5). The teacher should then draw to scale a smaller map of the area, hang it on the wall, and permit children to place buildings on the map (2, 3, 4, 5). Have the children locate their city or town on a simplified state map (1, 5, 6). Then refer them to a map of the United States to see where their state is located (1, 2, 3, 4, 5, 6).

THIRD GRADE

During a study of contrasting communities, children learn that people wear different clothes in different parts of the world. The relationship of this understanding to map interpretation is then presented. Pictures of people in typical dress for a particular time of year are placed on a map of the world that has a three color key—water, lowlands, and mountains (1, 5). People are placed, for example, on the equator, on lowlands and mountains, on a desert area, near the North Pole, and in the children's own community. Climatic conditions are estimated from the type of clothes worn and the effect of location on the climate (2, 3, 5, 6). The effect of altitude on climate and the resulting type of clothing is also interpreted. A representative relief map of clay or flour and salt is made to relate water, lowland, and mountains to the three color key (1, 5, 6).

FOURTH GRADE

Beginning a study of their state, the children use a large sand table to prepare a model representing the physical features of their state such as mountains, valleys, lakes, rivers, and lowlands (1, 2, 3, 5, 6). As the study progresses, the children can locate on the map major cities, their own city or town, recreational areas, and major products of the state (1, 2, 3, 4, 5, 6). The products and characteristics of an area located in the same latitude with approximately the same land formation should be compared (1, 3, 5, 6).

FIFTH GRADE

Fifth graders should use degrees of latitude and longitude for locating places. As children report daily news events from around the world, they should indicate the location of the event in degrees of latitude and longitude. The children can use individual desk maps to locate the places (1, 3, 4, 5). A world map with time zones designated is used to determine the time difference between the children's location and that of the event (1, 2, 3, 4, 5). The children interpret the map key representing physical features and relation of latitude to determine the land formation and climate of the news event's location (5, 6). The map key can also be used to interpret water formations or ocean currents that might be applicable to the event (5, 6).

SIXTH GRADE

During a study of the United Nations, committees of children can select areas of the world where United Nations organizations such as UNICEF, peace-keeping troops, and the economic advisory committee are operating. Reproduce maps of these areas with the opaque projector to insure accuracy (1, 2, 3, 6). Reproduce physical features using a five or seven color key (5, 6). These maps can be done on transparencies using overlays to represent political divisions, cities, physical features, products, and population (1, 2, 3, 4, 5, 6).

Other Suggested Activities

Because children need many concrete experiences to help them understand the concepts of map reading and interpretation, activities that can be used with various topics are suggested for both the primary and intermediate grades.

PRIMARY GRADES

Study the land formation around the school observing any variations and vegetation. Build a model of the area using clay or the sand table. Children in the upper-primary grades can refer to a physical map of the state to understand how the color key represents the land formation.

Plan a field trip to study local geographic features such as a river basin, rock formation, canyon, plateau, plain, or mountain. Observe them at different times of the year to note the effects of nature—the changing seasons, rain, wind, and snow.

Construct a globe using a balloon as the base. Place strips of papier-mâché over the balloon. When it dries, the balloon can be broken, and the land formations and water can be painted on the papier-mâché.

Children who are planning trips should study road maps and physical relief maps to anticipate land formations before they start their journey. They can follow the road map during the trip and share their experiences with the other children after they return.

Obtain aerial photos of different land formations and compare them with the same location on a geo-physical map.

INTERMEDIATE GRADES

Children should work with map construction frequently, especially when they are studying different areas of the world. Various materials can be used including plasticene clay, sawdust mixture, flour and salt, and papier-mâché. Children should develop a color key to indicate elevations.

The teacher can make sure that his students understand geographical terms such as "bay," "isthmus," "peninsula," etc. by helping them construct models of these physical features when they occur in the course of the study. Blank maps of the area under study are also helpful learning aids. As the study of an area progresses, each child can complete his map by drawing in the physical features, major cities, etc.

Children should be able to interpret many things from the information given on political and physical maps. When introducing a new area for study, before any preliminary reading or introduction has been made, the teacher should ask the children to suggest as much information about the area as possible from interpreting the map. In a study of cities, children should suggest geographic reasons for the locations of the cities.

Problems to Determine the Extent of Children's Skills

As children begin to acquire skills in map reading and interpretation, they should be presented with problem situations that require them to use the skills they have learned. The following problem example might be presented to kindergarten or first-grade children after they have learned directions and know where the sun rises and sets. The following picture is placed on a transparency:

Question:

If the sun is just rising, which way is the wind blowing?

This problem requires the children to think about the direction from which the sun rises and the resulting shadows. The bending of the tree indicates the direction of the wind.

As children learn to identify the types of products grown in different climatic and geographic regions, they should be able to describe conditions necessary for their growth. The teacher might present pictures of different types of vegetation and ask the children to name the type of climate and geographic conditions necessary for their growth.

The fact that the location rather than the physical appearance or natural resources of an area sometimes determines its importance offers an interesting problem for children to analyze. Some examples follow:

PLACE "A"

This is a chain of islands that covers in all an area of about 6,400 square miles. Some small shrubs and mosses grow here, but there are no trees. The climate is very cold and foggy. The population survives largely through fishing . . .

PLACE "B"

This is a rocky peninsula, which is largely a limestone "mountain" rising 1,400 feet above the water. It covers an area of about two square miles . . .

PLACE "C"

This is an island of volcanic origin. It is about 65 miles long and 2 to 18 miles wide. It has an area of about 463 square miles. Its climate is hot and humid, and it is subject to a large number of wind storms each . . .[4]

After a discussion of possible reasons for the importance of these places, the teacher can reveal their names—the Aleutian Islands, Gibraltar, and Okinawa.

When older children have a good grasp of the color key on a map and knowledge of the various theories about building a city, the following problem can be presented:

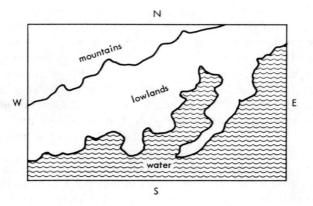

[4]Jan O. M. Broek, *Geography: Its Scope and Spirit* (Columbus, Ohio: Charles E. Merrill Publishing Co., 1965), p. 90.

Questions:

If you were to pick the site for a city in this area, where would you build it? Why?

This map should be presented on a transparency using a color key rather than words to distinguish the different physical features. The problem can be tackled individually or by the total class. The teacher may wish to add additional information about the natural resources, the winds, etc. The area shown is the Bay of Tokyo where the largest city in the world has been built.

Maps and Globes

Every elementary classroom should contain a globe. In kindergarten and first grade, a simple globe of slate or one that shows only the outline of the continents should be used. The slate globe can be drawn on with tempera or chalk and then washed or erased. Children should be permitted to manipulate the globe and to locate places such as their home and the United States. Reference to the globe by the teacher whenever feasible is important, for the children should form the habit of seeking it when the need arises.

Older children can use a more detailed globe—for example, the three- or five-color key of physical features can be used for the middle grades and a seven-color key for the intermediate grades. Use of a globe showing political boundaries with each country a different color has sometimes led children to believe that a country actually is the color shown on the globe. A globe that uses green for lowlands, brown for mountains, and blue for water might better orient children to globe usage.

Care should be exercised in the transition from globes to maps. The comparative size of Greenland is a good indicator of how shapes and sizes change from a globe to a map. Some map projections increase its size considerably while others decrease the size. The teacher might have the children split a tennis ball or the peel of an orange and attempt to flatten it completely to help them see what happens in the transition from a globe to a flat map.

Wall maps are generally not used before the end of second or third grade, depending upon the ability and background of the children. As indicated earlier, the first maps used should be homemade. Commercial maps should not contain too much detail to confuse the children. They should be large enough to be read easily across the classroom. Every upper-grade classroom should have a physical-political map of the world and, if money allows, physical-political maps of North America and other continents. Little use is made of separate physical and political maps, and the combination saves money.

A chart of geographical terms is a useful instructional tool for older children. This chart shows pictorially most of the geographic terms such as "isthmus," "harbor," "bay," and "plateau." These terms, however, should be taught as the need arises. They should not all be taught from the chart at one time.

The wall map of the world should be pulled down each day for ready reference. Games utilizing locational skills can be introduced during free play time—for example, a box with slips of paper containing places to be located might be kept by the map rack. Depending upon the grade level, various clues to the areas' locations can be added. Intermediate-grade children may use only the degrees of latitude and longitude for their reference.

To increase the children's understanding of the grid system, a simple demonstration can be completed. Place an "X" anywhere on the blackboard and have children tell exactly where it is located. Place several other "X's" on the board and give the same direction. Children soon realize that some additional reference points are needed. Draw horizontal lines several inches apart and number them. Problems still arise in determining the exact location until numbered vertical lines have been added. Children should readily associate this method with that used on maps and globes to increase accuracy in locating places.

Maps and globes can be purchased from a number of companies. The following list is representative of some of these companies. Catalogs can be secured upon request.

George F. Cram Co., Inc., 730 E. Washington Street, Indianapolis, Indiana 46206

Denoyer-Geppert Co., 5235 Ravenswood Avenue, Chicago, Illinois 60640

C. S. Hammond and Company, Inc., Maplewood, New Jersey 07040

Rand McNally and Company, P. O. Box 7800 Chicago, Illinois 60639

Map companies generally supply teachers with guides for instructional uses of their materials, and they also suggest lists of map and globe skills for each grade level.[5]

National Geographic Magazine supplies maps with each publication,

[5]Service Publication No. M44, Denoyer-Geppert Company, Chicago, Illinois.

but they usually contain too much detail for younger children. State chambers of commerce and embassies of foreign countries will provide maps of their areas. News magazines contain maps of areas where the news is happening. Weekly news maps with pictures of the events can be secured from *Time* magazine for a minimum charge.

SELECTED REFERENCES

Arnsdoff, Val, "Geographic Education: Principles and Practices in the Primary Grades," *Social Education*, XXXI (November, 1967), 612–14.

Carpenter, Helen McCracken, ed., *Skill Development in Social Studies*. Washington, D.C.: National Council for the Social Studies, 1963.

Drummond, Dorothy W., "Developing Geography Concepts in the Intermediate Grades," *Social Education*, XXX (December, 1966), 628–31.

Hanna, Paul R., Rose Sabaroff, and Gordon F. Davies, *Geography in the Teaching of Social Studies: Concepts and Skills*. Boston: Houghton Mifflin Company, 1966.

James, Preston E., ed., *New Viewpoints in Geography*. Washington, D.C.: National Council for the Social Studies, 1959.

Kennamer, Lorin, Jr., "Geography in the Middle Grades," *Social Education*, XXXI (November, 1967), 615–17.

Lee, John R. and Nathaniel Stampfer, "Two Studies in Learning Geography: Implications for the Primary Grades," *Social Education*, XXX (December, 1966), 627–28.

McAulay, John D., "Geography Understandings of the Primary Child," *Journal of Geography*, LV (April, 1966).

McAulay, John D., "What Understandings Do Second-Grade Children Have of Time Relationships?" *Journal of Educational Research*, LIV (1961), 312–14.

Rushdoony, Haig A., "Achievement in Map-Reading: An Experimental Study," *The Elementary School Journal*, LXIV (November, 1963), 70–75.

Does the manipulation of materials aid children in understanding concepts in social studies?

Utilization of Materials

A RICH AND INVITING SUPPLY OF MATERIALS IS AVAILABLE FOR use in social studies instruction. Fresh new materials enhance the social studies. The textbooks are colorful and appealing to children, films and filmstrips can be found to supplement almost any study, children's trade books add a spark of interest, realia kits present an opportunity to see the artifacts of a country, simulated games permit active involvement, and the vast amount of free and inexpensive materials provide extensive background information.

Part five discusses the selection and utilization of materials in elementary social studies with regard, when feasible, to the different methods of instruction.

CHAPTER ELEVEN

Utilization of Materials in the Social Studies

THE FOLLOWING DISCUSSION OF MATERIALS FOR USE IN THE social studies includes children's trade books, games, programmed materials, cartoons, graphs and charts, textbooks, multi-media kits, films and filmstrips, and free and inexpensive materials. These materials are representative but not exhaustive of those available.

Children's Trade Books

Two types of children's books can be incorporated with social studies—informational books that are primarily concerned with facts and fiction books that incorporate facts with hypothetical situations. May Hill Arbuthnot suggests that the following criteria be considered in selecting informational books:

1. *Scrupulous accuracy*—children have a tendency to accept what is in the book and therefore care should be exercised to check the accuracy of the information presented.
2. *Convenient presentation*—the information should be organized in such a way that children can easily find what they are looking for.
3. *Clarity*—little value will come from the information unless it is clearly stated for ease of understanding.
4. *Adequate treatment*—sufficient information should be included to insure understanding, but irrelevant details should not obscure the facts needed.
5. *Style*—an informational book should be interesting and as well written as possible.[1]

Informational books include titles such as Mabel Pyne's *The Little Geography of the United States*, which uses picture maps and colorful illustrations. *Landmark Books* is a series that is concerned with the various periods of development in the United States. Genevieve Foster's *George Washington's World*, *Abraham Lincoln's World*, and *Augustus Caesar's World* take a horizontal look at history to help children understand the events taking place in other parts of the world throughout the lifetime of each of these men. Both the *American Heritage Series* and *American Adventure Series* are written about the lives and events of famous people in American history. The *Childhood of Famous Americans Series* contains about one hundred selections dealing with people such as Abraham Lincoln, Booker T. Washington, and Babe Ruth. These stories begin with the individual's childhood and end during his adult life. The *We Were There Series* emphasizes dramatic events in our history. Any of these books can be used in research activities by individuals or committees. Role-playing and dramatic presentations are easily adapted from books about historical events or famous people.

People and Places by Margaret Mead discusses anthropological concepts of the similarities and differences among peoples of the world and offers suggestions that might solve man's problems so all may live together peacefully. *Why We Live Where We Live* by Eva Knox Evans presents geographical information about the United States and the interdependence of people. Her final chapter "Your Own Home Town" encourages the reader to seek information about his own community.

For the child who has an aversion to geography and history, fiction books by Holling C. Holling's *Paddle-to-the-Sea* or *Tree in the Trail* should prove fascinating as well as educational. *Tree in the Trail* presents the history of our westward movement through the experiences of a cottonwood tree on the Santa Fe Trail. *Paddle-to-the-Sea* is the story

[1]May Hill Arbuthnot, *Children and Books* (Chicago: Scott, Foresman and Company, 1964), pp. 565–66.

of a small carved canoe containing the figure of an Indian. The canoe is set to float from the Upper Great Lakes to make its way to the sea. These books contain accurate geographical and historical material presented in a way that should interest children and motivate them to learn more about the topics under consideration.

Depicting the forces of change, Virginia Lee Burton's *The Little House* finds itself in a country setting until the growth of the surrounding area overwhelms it and a city grows up around it. Intended for young children, this book can be used with a study of the local community.

Children who read Marguerite DeAngeli's *Bright April* are provided with a much better understanding of and feeling for improving racial relations. Lois Lenski is another author who has described the lives of children in various parts of our country. *Strawberry Girl* and *Cotton in My Sack* were written about farm workers in Florida and Arkansas. Her *Prairie School* discusses the hard life of the plains states.

Books about children from other lands such as May McNeer's *The Mexican Story*, which provides descriptions of accounts in the history of that country, or *Nine Days to Christmas*, which gives an account of the customs of the country, are useful when studying other cultures. Folktales of our own and other countries provide an excellent introduction to the study of other areas. Children are fascinated to learn why certain traditions have withstood the passing of time.

These children's books add a touch of interest and uniqueness to social studies that cannot be found in any other resource. Many other fine books too numerous to mention can readily be used in social studies. Helen Huus' *Children's Books to Enrich the Social Studies* is an excellent resource.

Games

Recently, relatively new materials have been developed for the social studies classroom. They are labeled "simulation," "simulation games," or just "games." Hermann, in the *Encyclopedia of the Social Sciences*, defines simulation as a situation having human players and rules and outcomes that are sufficiently elaborate to require the use of calculators or computers. Games are more simplistic, more manual, and less amenable to computer analysis. Simulated games are situations in which the less sophisticated may "assume the roles of decision-makers in a simulated (imitated) environment according to specified procedures or rules."[2]

[2]*Simulation Games for the Social Studies Classroom* (New York: Foreign Policy Association, 1968), p. 9.

No specific rules have been established for designing simulated games, but elements that might be involved in them are suggested:

1. Identification of objectives—what will be learned by the game?
2. Construction of a simplified model of the process or system that will best serve the objectives.
3. Identification of the various actors or teams so that the number would demonstrate the model effectively and also conform to classroom needs.
4. Provision of resources for the players to exchange in competition with other players.
5. Establishing rules or limits of permissible behavior during the game.
6. Identification of objectives or goals for the actors as they engage in trading resources.
7. Development of a scene or setting the stage for the beginning of play.[3]

The exciting aspect of simulation games is their involvement of the children, who actively participate in decision-making, diplomatic maneuvers, or some other equally stimulating experience. Most children enjoy these simulation games, which are believed to be educational. Because there are no hard-and-fast rules for game design, teachers and students can produce their own games, utilizing the previously discussed elements. Four games that were developed for a sixth-grade classroom are: *Inflation* —simulates the inflation of a money system; *Production Line*—"demonstrates the greater efficiency of the production line as compared to the output of individual craftsmen;"[4] *Landlocked Nations*—demonstrates "why nations through history have been willing to fight for control of narrow waterways;"[5] *Parent-Satellite Nations*—helps children gain insight into the development of a nation from a satellite to a power in its own right.

There are several commercially-produced games for elementary-school classrooms, but more are available at junior, senior, and adult levels. *Caribou Hunting* and *Seal Hunting*, elementary-school games, are both board games in which students simulate some of the difficulties Eskimos experience in acquiring an adequate food supply.[6] *Consumer* is designed to teach something about the problems and economics of installment buying.[7] *Market* aids children in the acquisition of the concepts of supply,

[3]*Simulation Games for the Social Studies Classroom*, p. 114.
[4]Charles and Dorothy Christine, "Four Simulation Games That Teach," *Grade Teacher*, October, 1967, p. 112. Reprinted from *Grade Teacher* Magazine by permission of the publishers. Copyright October 1967 by Teachers Publishing Corporation.
[5]Christine, "Four Simulation Games That Teach," p. 114.
[6]Education Development Center, 15 Miflin Place, Cambridge, Massachusetts 02138.
[7]The Johns Hopkins University, Department of Social Relations, Baltimore, Maryland 21218.

demand, and prices.[8] *Sierra Leone* and the *Sumerian Game* are both computer-based games in economics.[9] "The child makes decisions and enters his answers at the computer terminal"[10] and immediately receives a progress report.

"Proponents of simulation and games in social studies education claim that intuitive thinking is developed, learning is made entertaining and relevant to student life experiences. Emphasis is placed on developing analytical approaches and organizing concepts transferable to other problems."[11]

Certainly more research is needed in this area, but teachers can experiment in their own classrooms to determine the success of games with their students. Do the games improve intuitive thinking? Are children more interested in learning? Do they learn as much?

One area that particularly needs exploring is that of the lasting effect of game-playing on children. Does it change values? Does it increase competitiveness? What effect does the power to manipulate the lives of others, assumed in a game, have upon children? These are questions that require answers before the effectiveness of games can be determined.

Programmed Material

The objective of programmed material is to give the learner elements of a subject in sequential order. This material provides immediate feedback for the learner, who then knows whether his answer is correct or incorrect. Many programmed materials require review before the learner can go on, if an incorrect answer is given. The success of achieving correct answers is expected to motivate the learner to continue the study.

Programmed materials are available in several forms—programmed textbooks, teaching machines, and computer programs. In programmed textbooks, answers to questions either appear on another page or are covered by a flap on the same page. Teaching machines are found in a variety of forms such as the Cyclo Teacher of *Encyclopedia Britannica*, which hides the answer until the children move to the next question, or computer-based systems, which assess children's answers and present information for their next step.

[8]Industrial Relations Center, University of Chicago, Chicago, Illinois.

[9]Board of Cooperative Educational Services, Westchester County, Yorktown Heights, New York 10598.

[10]*Simulation Games for the Social Studies Classroom*, p. 21.

[11]Leonard W. Ingraham, "Teachers, Computers, and Games: Innovations in the Social Studies," *Social Education*, XXXI (January, 1967), 53.

The potential of programmed materials has not been realized, especially in the area of computerized instruction. The research completed to date has not determined what type of material is best presented by programming.

Few programmed materials have been produced for elementary school. Some examples of those in use are *Learning To Use A Globe Set I and II* by Ewing and Seibel, which is a scrambled text to teach global concepts. A programmed text for teaching about maps is *Geography of the United States* by MacGraw and Williams. *An Introduction To American Government* by Rosenhack illustrates the separation of powers in our Federal Government. The latter two texts are for use in the upper-elementary grades.

Cartoons

Cartoons are best used to stimulate discussions, present a particular point of view, and provide an opportunity to interpret the opinion of others. Most cartoons use symbols that require previous experience to be understood. If children lack this experience, teachers should assist in the interpretation.

Criteria for selecting cartoons for instruction include:

Does the cartoon present an idea quickly and effectively?

Does it present an idea that would be difficult to introduce using a different approach?

Will it be understood by the majority of the students without too much assistance?

Cartoons that might embarrass children of a certain race, religion, or national origin, unless the discussion to be initiated concerns prejudice or a controversial issue, should be avoided. Frequently, a cartoon expresses a view of a controversial issue better than most methods.

To enable all of the children in a class to see a cartoon at the same time, the teacher should transfer it to a transparency for the overhead projector or mount it for the opaque projector. Children should be encouraged to collect cartoons that provoke thought. These cartoons can be used in school for committee presentations or individual reports. Children delight in developing their own cartoons. This activity aids them in understanding the subtle use of symbols.

The following cartoons are examples that should effectively provoke discussion.

"Boon to mankind, ha! One of these days it'll get loose and burn up the whole world."

*"Filibuster or no filibuster, I don't want my secret recipes
in the Congressional Record!"*

°Gurney Williams, ed., *Look on the light side* (Englewood Cliffs, N.J.: Prentice-Hall, Inc., 1957), reprinted from *Look* Magazine.
    †Gurney Williams, ed., *Look on the light side, Ibid.*

Teacher: What idea is the first cartoon attempting to portray?

The next cartoon quickly presents an idea. The idea presented however, is one that children might not readily perceive.

Teacher: What does this cartoon suggest happens during a filibuster in Congress?

Many cartoons are too sophisticated for young children, but occasionally an appropriate one will be found. No doubt, the most valuable result of using cartoons in social studies is to provide children with greater ability to interpret them as adults. Also, the reluctant learner may be motivated about a topic by the use of cartoons when otherwise he would be disinterested.

Graphs and Charts

Just as cartoons can present certain ideas more effectively, graphs and charts can often be used to illustrate an idea or present information more readily than other methods. Children who have difficulty with reading may interpret a graph or chart successfully and acquire the concept that others read.

It is necessary to assist children in learning to read and interpret graphs and charts. Young children should start with picture graphs that are related to something familiar to them. An example is Graph 1, which uses stick figures to indicate the lunch count for the day.

GRAPH 1. Room 10 lunch count

Each child can readily perceive how he is represented on the graph. Children may wish to label the graph with their names to be sure that all are represented. Later, the teacher can explain that it is possible to represent several people with one figure as shown in Graph 2.

GRAPH 2. Room 10 lunch count

Bar graphs in the classroom can be used to represent the daily temperatures as shown in Graph 3.

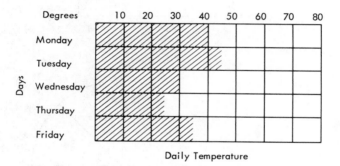

GRAPH 3. Daily temperature

After the children can interpret the bar graph, line graphs, illustrated by Graph 4, can be introduced using the same information as the bar graph for comparison and ease of understanding.

Circle graphs, illustrated by Graph 5, are easily understood when they are used to show how a pie might be divided among the children.

Preparation of graphs using information related to classroom experiences during early primary grades will provide children with the understanding necessary to tackle the more abstract statistics presented in the middle and upper grades. Correct labeling of the graphs is vital, and emphasis should be placed on reading them accurately.

A variety of charts are found in every elementary classroom. Most children are introduced to school activities through the use of experience charts. Here, a mutual class experience is recorded using the children's description for all to read. Charts are also developed to record the rules of a game, the directions for committee work, and the helpers for the week.

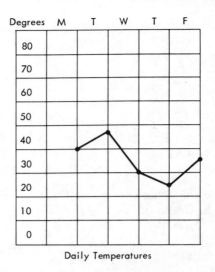

GRAPH 4. Daily temperature

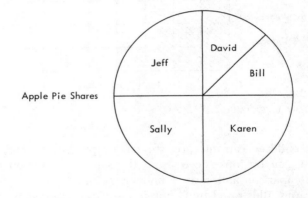

GRAPH 5. Apple pie shares

A chart with pictures (for example, one depicting the process of making paper from the cutting of a tree until the finished product) is called a flow chart. These charts aid in understanding the steps involved in a process. In the primary grades, children can be introduced to them by using the book *Pelle's New Suit*, which describes how Pelle obtains a new suit from the time he shears wool from the sheep until he picks up his suit at the tailor's shop. Young children can draw and interpret a flow chart of the process described in this book. More complicated processes such as drilling and refining oil can be understood by older children.

Commercial flow charts are available on legislative processes such as "How a Bill Becomes a Law" or manufacturing processes such as "Milk from the Farm to You."

Charts can be used for comparison—comparing the before and after, past and present, or another country's government with ours. A chart is described as a pictorial or line diagram of a topic.

Textbooks

A prime source material for the social studies is the textbook. Frequently, it is the basis or guide for the organization of instruction in the classroom. For this reason, care should be exercised in selecting textbooks. The following criteria of selection are suggested:

1. Is the organization of the textbook easily followed?
2. Are the concepts presented in a manner that most students will be able to understand?
3. Are there sufficient illustrations, maps, charts, and graphs to increase the reader's understanding?
4. Does the text contain a table of contents, index, and sufficient appendices to aid the reader in locating information?
5. Are references listed where additional information can be secured such as films, books, records, etc.?
6. Is there a teacher's guide with suggestions concerning uses of the text in instruction?
7. Does the text contain a multi-ethnic presentation of topics?
8. Are the authors respected scholars from the social sciences and social studies education?

UTILIZATION

For too long, the textbook has been used by too many teachers as a crutch in teaching social studies. This practice is exemplified by the teacher who, whether unprepared for the lesson or lacking an understanding of teaching principles, has each student read a text paragraph orally and then discusses the concepts. The underachieving reader does not benefit from the oral reading, and the more capable reader is bored. Several other techniques would better utilize the resources of the text. A sample lesson plan follows:

Topic: Mexico.

Objective: To understand the culture of Mexico by acquiring knowledge of its historical development.

Materials: Textbook, study guide, and visual aids.

Procedure: Group I, Underachievers—Use a textbook that contains a physical-political map of Mexico, a historical map of early Spanish explorations, and a story of Cortez's capture of the Aztecs. Use realia of Mexico including a record of Spanish and Mexican Indian language, dolls dressed in native Mexican dress, pottery, and musical instruments.

1. Using the maps in the textbook, discuss the location of Mexico in relation to the United States and its geographical areas. Using the historical map, trace the routes of the Spanish explorers to Mexico.
2. Read the story of Cortez's explorations and conquest of the Aztecs to the children. Observe the realia of the country and discuss how the Spanish conquest influenced its culture.

Group II, Average Achievers—Have the children read silently the chapter on Spanish exploration and conquest in Mexico. Establish a purpose for the reading with the following study guide questions.

1. Try to determine the reasons why Spanish explorers were interested in the New World, particularly Mexico.
2. Trace the route of Cortez in Mexico and discuss the type of problems the physical features and climate gave his men.
3. Why was Cortez able to defeat the Aztecs?

Group III, Above Average—Use the same study guide as above with these additional activities and questions.

1. Read another account of the Spanish conquest from a different resource and compare the two descriptions.
2. Are there any discrepancies in the accounts?
3. If so, why would this difference occur?
4. Discuss what you think Mexico would be like if the French or English had conquered the Aztecs.

In this sample lesson plan, all groups utilize the text, but each with a different level of abstraction.

The textbook can be used by committees for exploratory reading or research information. The suggested references included in the textbook provide excellent resources for extending research activities. The textbook can also be used for individual or group research in a problem-solving situation. Textbooks have been criticized because too many of the situations they present describe life in suburbia and fail to interest children who come from disadvantaged homes. Today, many textbook series are attempting to alleviate this problem.

Beginning teachers find the guide to the textbook invaluable for suggested teaching techniques, instructional activities, and additional resources. The danger in the guide lies in the teacher's failure to adapt the use of the text and guide to the needs of the children in a particular classroom.

Multi-Media Kits

Media materials organized around a major topic have been assembled into kits for use in social studies instruction.[12] These kits contain films, filmstrips, records, realia, written information, and a teacher's guide to instruction. International Communications Foundation has assembled these kits for the study of other cultures. Many kits are available for countries such as Pakistan, Afghanistan, and Turkey, for which it is often difficult to find sufficient information at the children's level.

Examples of the materials available for Mexico are films of the life of the people, filmstrips on aspects of the culture, records of the language and stories, and realia including dolls dressed in the native dress, pieces of clothing, and musical instruments. Also included is the teacher's guide with background information and suggested teaching techniques for use of the materials.

The advantage in using kits such as these lies in the accessibility of materials—many of the items included would be rather difficult for teachers to obtain. Because some children will learn more from handling realia than from viewing a filmstrip about the items, use of the different media helps meet individual differences in the classroom.

These kits can be used with several teaching methods. Individual or committee research can be organized around the materials for unit teaching or problem solving. Because disadvantaged children benefit from concrete materials, the kits can be used successfully with them. The kits can also be presented to the entire class as introduction to a new study or for enrichment. More of these kits will soon be available.[13]

Films and Filmstrips

Films and filmstrips provide visual representations instead of the abstract representations provided by text descriptions. Both sources of in-

[12]International Communications Foundation, 9033 Wilshire Boulevard, Beverly Hills, California.

[13]*Educational Media Guide* (New York: The Educational Media Council, 1963).

formation are important and must be carefully chosen. Criteria to be applied in the selection of every film or filmstrip include:

1. Is there continuity of content throughout the film or filmstrip?
2. Is the photography of good quality?
3. Is the sound of the film easily understood?
4. Will the presentation of the film or filmstrip contribute to the understanding of the topic under study?
5. Is the information presented accurate?
6. Can the information be understood by elementary school children?

Films and filmstrips should be selected on the basis of their best use. Does the film introduce a new topic effectively? Does it provide background information? Does it motivate interest in a topic? Would it be effective as a culmination to a study? Guides are available to aid teachers in selecting films and filmstrips.[14]

Effective presentation and follow-up of films and filmstrips is vital if they are to be worthwhile. An introduction to the film or filmstrip should establish some purpose for viewing them. Study-guide questions can be provided or oral discussions can be conducted to introduce the film or filmstrip. Follow-up after the viewing is necessary to clarify understanding and reinforce learning. Children can evaluate the effectiveness of the presentation.

Free and Inexpensive Materials

The teacher can obtain an abundance of free or inexpensive materials, which can aid considerably in social studies instruction. Travel agencies and transportation companies such as airlines, railways, and trucking industries supply teachers with posters and charts of places to visit and with booklets that explain the transportation systems. These packets may also have background information for the teacher.

Chambers of commerce in cities and states and embassies of countries provide extensive information about their areas. They often include maps and colorful posters and regulations for travel in their areas.

A variety of manufacturing, publishing, packing, and insurance com-

[14]*Education Film Guide* (H. W. Wilson, 950 University Avenue, New York City, New York 10052).

panies have educational materials that they supply to teachers upon request. Agencies of the United States government provide materials at a small charge. Several guides are available with information about securing these materials.[15]

Pictures and information from magazines and newspapers often add resources for the study of a topic. Teachers should start a file of these resources for use when needed. To be easily accessible, the file should be divided into possible topics of study. Slides, photographs, and postcards collected from the teacher's own travels should also be added as resources.

SELECTED REFERENCES

Boocock, Sarane S., ed., *Simulation Games in Learning*. Beverly Hills, Calif.: Sage Publishers, 1968.

Fraser, Dorothy M., ed., "Review of Curriculum Materials," *Social Education*, XXXII (April, 1968), 362–85.

Free and Inexpensive Learning Materials (14th ed.). Nashville, Tennessee: George Peabody College for Teachers, 1968.

Hogan, Arthur J., "Simulation: An Annotated Bibliography," *Social Education*, XXXII (March, 1968), 242–44.

Ingraham, Leonard W., "Teachers, Computers, and Games: Innovations in the Social Studies," *Social Education*, XXXI (January, 1967), 51–53.

Joyce, Bruce R., *Strategies for Elementary Social Science Education*. Chicago: Science Research Associates, 1965.

Rader, William, "Yes—But What Is Available?" *Social Education*, XXXII (January, 1968), 57–59.

Rice, Marion, "Materials for Teaching Anthropology in the Elementary School," *Social Education*, XXXII (March, 1968), 254–56.

Source Directory Single Concept Films, Technicolor Commercial and Educational Division, 1300 Frowley Drive, Costa Mesa, California 92627.

Walsh, Huber M., "Learning Resources for Individualizing Instruction," *Social Education*, XXXI (May, 1967), 413.

[15]*Educators' Progress Service* (Randolph, Wisconsin 53956) publishes *Educators' Guide to Free Films, Educators' Guide to Free Filmstrips, Educators' Guide to Free Social Studies Materials, Educators' Guide to Free Teaching Aids,* and *Educators' Index to Free Materials.*

Does the behavior of children indicate the success of the instruction?

Evaluation

Was the program of instruction in social studies successful? Were the teaching techniques effective? Have the objectives of the social studies program been achieved? Have the children acquired skill in intuitive thinking, problem solving, and developing human relationships? These are some of the questions that teachers ask themselves about the outcomes of their social studies instruction. How can they determine the answers to these questions? What evaluation techniques are effective for different aspects of the program? Will the method of instruction affect the evaluation techniques?

Part six discusses methods and techniques of evaluation used at the national, state, local, and classroom level.

CHAPTER TWELVE

Evaluation of Social Studies Instruction

EVALUATION OF INSTRUCTION AT ANY LEVEL IS ACCOMPLISHED by measuring the extent to which established objectives have been achieved. The objectives state the expected outcome of a learning experience. The technique of evaluation that best determines if the objectives have been reached must be selected. The primary purpose of evaluation is to determine the progress achieved and, when necessary, to initiate changes for the improvement of instruction.

The focus of emphasis of evaluation, however, might shift at the different levels—classroom, local, state, and national. The teacher in the classroom is concerned about Johnny and his success in getting along with the committee members, while local, state, and national concern is more global —can all the Johnnys and Marys operate cooperatively in society? At each level, objectives are established on the basis of a philosophy of education. Then, utilizing various evaluation techniques, the success with which these objectives or goals have been met is determined. It is possible that different techniques of evaluation will be used at each level.

Evaluation of instruction in the classroom must be continuous and it must encompass all learning experiences. A teacher should ask himself these questions as he plans learning experiences. How will this experience benefit the children? What objective will this experience achieve? Too often teachers are not certain of what should be evaluated or of the standards of evaluation to be used. The teacher must establish goals for social studies instruction for the entire year, and he must attempt to select daily or weekly experiences that will lead to the attainment of these overall goals. Obviously, evaluation is necessary throughout the teaching-learning process and it is particularly important at these points: (1) evaluation of a single learning experience; (2) evaluation of a group of experiences organized around a unit of study, a problem-solving situation, or the presentation of concepts from the social sciences; and (3) longitudinal evaluation of the progress achieved over a period of time whether a month, semester, or year.

At each point in the educational program, the teacher establishes objectives or goals, provides learning experiences for the children, and then evaluates the extent to which the objectives have been achieved. The evaluation involves several facets—the success of the teaching technique, the materials utilized, and the attainment of the objectives. Figure 8 illustrates this process.

FIGURE 8. Process of evaluation.

The learning experience should be evaluated in terms of (1) the achievement of the goal or objective and (2) the effectiveness of the teaching-learning process and the materials utilized. It is important to determine how the goal was reached as well as whether or not it was reached.

If objectives have been stated in behavioral or performance terms, the teacher can evaluate the learning experience more easily. An example (given in chapter one) of a cognitive objective stated in behavioral terms is:

To list at least one of the Mexican holidays that is different from those celebrated in the United States.

This knowledge can be evaluated by an objective test item or an essay question. The teacher knows exactly what he expects of the children.

An example of an affective objective stated in behavioral terms is:

To value the contributions the many subcultures have made to our heritage and express an appreciation for them.

Again, the teacher knows exactly what is to be evaluated. He can observe the children at work and play and note their comments concerning other cultures or he can use a questionnaire to determine each child's attitudes.

Readily acknowledged is the difficulty of evaluating the affective domain (attitudes of children) versus the cognitive (thinking) domain. Obviously, a measurement of the knowledge or understanding gained through instruction can be more easily obtained (through objective or essay tests, discussions, and conferences) than can a measurement of the attitudes acquired or changed by the instruction. Successful evaluation, however, requires that multiple methods be used to complete the total picture of the instruction's achievement. Observation, a checklist, and conferences may help the teacher assess attitudes; an objective test reveals the amount of knowledge gained; and an essay test, group discussion, or conference indicates the amount of understanding obtained. Each method contributes its data to complete the complicated task of evaluation.

Methods of Evaluation

OBSERVATION

In the classroom, the teacher uses the method of observation most frequently to evaluate learning experiences. As he conducts a discussion, the teacher observes the expressions on the children's faces. Are they interested? Which children are always ready with the answers? Are there shy children who never enter the discussion? Do the children appear to understand? Would another method of instruction be more effective? During committee participation, the teacher observes the children working together. Are they willing to share? Do all children participate in the decision-making? Does each child complete his work on time? Because it is often difficult to remember the answers to these questions for each child, teachers find it necessary to develop a record for reference. The most common method used is a checklist of the objectives of the learning experience, on which the teacher records each child's success or failure in achieving the objectives. A sample checklist follows:

	Willing to Share	Listens to Others	Completes Work on Time	Expresses his Opinion	Possesses Creative Ideas	
1. Kay	U	U	O	O	O	
2. Bill	O	S	S	U	U	
3. Rita	S	S	S	S	S	
4. Gay	O	O	O	O	O	

O   Outstanding
S   Satisfactory
U   Unsatisfactory

Another method of recording on a checklist involves keeping a separate sheet for each child, for example:

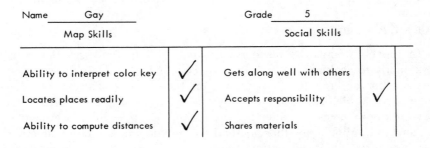

Name   Gay   Grade   5

    Map Skills   Social Skills

Ability to interpret color key	✓	Gets along well with others	
Locates places readily	✓	Accepts responsibility	✓
Ability to compute distances	✓	Shares materials	

Use of the checklist facilitates observation and makes it more systematic. The checklist provides the teacher with definite behaviors to observe and a valuable record for use in reporting the children's progress.

CONFERENCES

The opportunity to converse with a child on a one-to-one basis is often a revealing form of evaluation. Attitudes, understandings, and interests may be assessed by this method. Certain guidelines should be followed while conducting an individual conference: (1) Identify the goal of the conference—for example, direct the conference toward learning about the child's attitude toward people of another culture. (2) Prepare questions and discuss them during the conference—for example, If you were to take a trip anywhere in the world, where would you go? Why? (3) Establish good rapport with the child as soon as possible—discuss some personal event, a game, an interest. (4) Listen carefully to what the child has to say and make notations about the child's answers after the completion of the conference. (5) Leave the conference with a word of encouragement to the child and a definite plan of action.

The child should be prepared for the conference and have his own goals and questions in mind. Before the conference, he might ask himself: Are there questions I want to ask? Do I understand what we are studying? Does the teacher have suggestions for the improvement of my work? Do I have any projects or research I want to complete? If children have a thorough understanding of the purpose of the conference, it will be more profitable for them and their teacher.

Individual conferences can also be used for oral testing. The child who has difficulty with reading or the child who has a mental block about tests can have the test administered in a conference situation.

Individual conferences are open to criticism, especially if the class is large, because of their time consuming nature. However, five or ten minutes spent with an individual child is well worth the time in terms of the results. In addition to obtaining the intended evaluation, the teacher will also get to know the child and he may be able to spot possible problem areas. Ten minutes in an individual conference could help solve a problem for a child that might otherwise go unnoticed. In the conference, the teacher also has the opportunity to guide the child toward self-evaluation with questions such as: Are you satisfied with your work? Do you think you could do better? What do you see as your problems? The number of individual conferences held will depend upon their success, their intended purpose, the children's reactions, and the teacher's schedule.

The total class or small groups such as a committee can evaluate a mutual experience. This type of session permits a child to compare his or his group's performance with the performances of others and to assess his role in the total group process. In this situation, children should learn the role of constructive criticism. This example of a group discussion following the presentation of an oral report by a committee of sixth graders illustrates these values.

TEACHER. As we look at the guidelines for presenting an oral report, how well do you think Kim's group followed them?

JERRY. I didn't think the report was very good.

SANDY. Me, neither.

TEACHER. What is our first rule in evaluating someone else's work?

JERRY. Look for something that was well done and comment on that.

TEACHER. Yes, and if we criticize their work, what should we include?

SANDY. We should tell what was wrong and how it might be improved.

TEACHER. Right, shall we try again.

JUAN. The group used pictures to illustrate their talk, which made it easier to understand.

KATHY. Yes, and the art work was so beautiful.

MURPHY. Some of the members of the group did not speak out so we all could hear and that spoiled their report.

SID. If they had moved out in front of the table, it would have been easier to hear them.

In this example, the teacher quickly turned what might have been a useless evaluation session into positive constructive criticism.

In another group session, the children might evaluate the behavior and performance of the group on a field trip and the value of the trip. The teacher would ask for comments on general behavior and request that children refrain from pinpointing individual actions that might embarrass the children involved. In assessing the value of the field trip, the childern compare what they learned with the goals that were previously established for the trip.

Group discussions can be conducted daily to evaluate topics such as groups working together, the effectiveness of materials utilized, or the children's understanding of a film, outside speaker, or a reading. Such discussion aids teachers in determining the effectiveness of a particular teaching technique. Through discussion and comparison of the work completed by individuals and groups, these sessions also lead the child toward introspection and evaluation of his own behavior and achievement.

TEACHER-MADE TESTS

The type of test a teacher devises depends upon: (1) what he is attempting to evaluate and (2) his method of instruction. For example, the teacher who has presented purely factual information would not give an essay test that evaluates understanding. It is advantageous for a teacher to prepare his own test, for he can then base the test questions on the things he deems most valuable for evaluation.

Essay tests can present problem-solving situations, determine understanding, and assess attitudes. The reliability of scoring an essay test is questioned, however, and the time required to score such tests is listed as a disadvantage.

Objective tests can test a wider variety of topics and they are more easily scored, but they require more time in planning and writing than the essay test. The Educational Testing Service suggests the following steps in preparing an objective test:

Step   1 List the major topics covered in your particular teaching unit. This list should not exceed five.
Step   2 Indicate the number of items you want to devote to each topic.
Step   3 List under each topic the things you want students to know about, understand, or be able to do.
Step   4 Collect materials on which to base items. (Textual material—typed or read by teacher, pictorial material, music, or specimens to be examined).[1]
Step   5 Begin writing of the items for your test.
Step   6 Submit the items for review by another individual.
Step   7 Rewrite or replace defective items.
Step   8 Arrange the items into a test. May be arranged from easy to hard or by common subject matter.
Step   9 Prepare directions for the test.
Step 10 Prepare an answer key.[2]

Different test elements that can be included are: (1) completion, (2) alternative response, (3) multiple choice, (4) matching, and (5) rearrangement.

CHILD SELF-EVALUATION

One of the goals of instruction in any subject area is that of self-evaluation. The child who can look at his progress objectively and discuss

[1]Educational Testing Service, Cooperative Test Division, Princeton, New Jersey. *Making Your Own Tests*, p. 15.
[2]*Making Your Own Tests*, pp. 1–7.

his strengths and weaknesses has achieved a valuable goal. Checklists based on the objectives of social studies are helpful, for they allow children to record their achievement. The process of asking himself questions about his activities aids the child in self-evaluation. Examples of items for such checklists are:

1. Do I try to do my best work?
2. Do I look carefully at all sides of an issue?
3. Do I enjoy working with others?
4. Do I listen carefully to what others have to say?
5. Do I respect others who are different from me?

Another method of self-evaluation involves keeping a record of a series of experiences, for example, in a diary or log. As the child records a description of the activities, he should be encouraged to discuss his role and the degree to which he achieved the goal he had established for himself. Children, too, need to realize that there are limitations to their abilities and that they should not set unrealistic goals for themselves.

LOCAL

Evaluation of social studies instruction by the school district is generally accomplished through standardized achievement tests, evaluation by committees of teachers, and self-evaluation by individual teachers. Standardized tests are administered to determine the children's achievement as compared to the norm for selected groups across the nation. Care should be exercised in interpreting these tests, because children in a specific school may vary considerably in socio-economic status, experiential background, and intelligence from the groups on which the norms are based. These test results should not be used to compare the teachers' competency nor the pupils' achievement from year to year. These tests do, however, indicate areas of instruction (for example, map-reading skills or sequential relationships) in which groups of children score low and, therefore, need additional instruction.

The *Sixth Mental Measurements Yearbook* provides information about the most recently published tests. This information includes a discussion of the test, price, and publisher. *Tests in Print* is another resource that briefly describes all tests available.

A selected list of standardized achievement tests for elementary school follows:

Sequential Tests of Educational Progress: Social Studies, 1963, Grades 4–6. Cooperative Test Division, Educational Testing Service.

Stanford Achievement Test: Intermediate and Advanced Social Studies, Grades 5–9, 1954 (New York: Harcourt, Brace & World, Inc., 1954).

Metropolitan Achievement Tests: Social Studies, Grades 5–6, 1964 (New York: Harcourt, Brace & World, Inc., 1964).

Committees of teachers selected across school and grade levels are frequently assigned the task of evaluating the social studies program for the school district. On the basis of the established objectives, they may develop evaluation forms to be used in observing classrooms. The observation forms may be completed by administrators or teacher members of the committee during a visit in the classroom. The disadvantage of this method of evaluation is the limited time available for observation in each classroom.

Teacher self-evaluation forms may also be developed to be completed by individual teachers. This type of evaluation gives the teacher the opportunity to evaluate his program of instruction in terms of the standards established by the school district. If such a self-evaluation form is not a part of the school district evaluation, a teacher may devise his own checklist. An extensive self-analysis checklist can be found in *A Guide for the Elementary Social Studies Teacher*.[3]

More recently, evaluation has been attempted through the use of videotaping, interaction analysis, and team-teaching observation. Use of a portable videotape machine permits televising of a segment of the instruction conducted in the classroom. Preserving the experience on tape allows the teacher to view the lesson later by himself or with a supervisor to determine its effectiveness.

Interaction analysis has been researched by numerous educators including Marie Hughes, B. Othaniel Smith, Donald Medley and Harold Mitzel, John Withall, and Ned Flanders. Category systems have been developed to classify verbal interaction in the classroom. These systems consist of the establishment of basic categories for teacher talk, student talk, and silence to determine the amount and type of verbal interaction. Tape recordings of class sessions can be made for later categorization of the verbal interaction, or trained observers can use the category systems during live sessions. Most researchers emphasize that these systems are not directed toward evaluation per se, but rather toward the improvement of instruction. Their aim is to move away from teacher-talk dominated instruction toward more verbal interaction from the students.

Team-teaching situations permit evaluation of instruction in group sessions by team members. As one member of the team is presenting a lesson, other team members can observe and analyze the results of the

---

[3]W. Linwood Chase, *A Guide for the Elementary Social Studies Teacher* (Boston: Allyn & Bacon, Inc., 1966), pp. 196–206.

instruction. Close faculty cooperation is necessary to permit open discussion of the methods and techniques used during the teaching. Self-evaluation can also be accomplished by a team member as he observes a fellow team member teaching.

At the state level, the primary purpose for evaluation is to determine the extent of curriculum revision necessary, if any. Previously mentioned, the state of Oregon divided the state into ten regional districts for pre-evaluation before attempting any revision. California organized a State-wide Social Science Study Committee, which includes classroom teachers and social science educators, to analyze the social studies curriculum of the state. The most recent Progress Report of March, 1968 presents the abridgement of the new curriculum. Other states that have extensive curriculum revision projects are Minnesota, Wisconsin, Indiana, New York, and Connecticut.

NATIONAL

Evaluation of instructional programs has been undertaken at the national level in recent years. Different groups of teachers, scholars, and curriculum specialists from across the nation have been engaged to develop instruments of evaluation. The National Assessment of American Education, a study funded by the United States government, states as its purpose "to find out what Americans know, believe, and are able to do. It is an attempt to find out about such attainments in most fields of study considered important in American schools; for example, reading, language arts, science, mathematics, social studies, citizenship, fine arts, and vocational education."[4] Notice that social studies and citizenship education are to be assessed separately.

Before test items were written, the objectives of social studies education were developed. These objectives were formulated by a panel of scholars, teachers, and curriculum specialists and were submitted to a panel of citizens for approval. Five major objectives were established:

1. Within the limits of his maturity, a person competent in the area of social studies uses analytic, scientific procedures effectively.
2. A person competent in the area of social studies has knowledge relevant to the major ideas and concerns of social scientists.
3. He has a reasonable commitment to the values that sustain a free society.
4. He has curiosity about human affairs.
5. He is sensitive to creative-intuitive methods of explaining the condition.[5]

[4]Dana Kurfman, "A National Assessment of Social Studies Education," *Social Education*, XXXI (March, 1967), 210–11.
[5]"A National Assessment of Social Studies Education," pp. 210–11.

"On the basis of these objectives, a series of test items will be devised for varying age levels. Interviews, free response, and questionnaires will also be utilized. Data will be obtained for boys and girls, geographic regions, four age groups; 9, 13, 17 year-olds, and adults; urban, suburban, and rural, and two socioeconomic levels."[6] Concern has been expressed that this evaluation will be used to compare school districts, schools, and teachers. But because the data will be compiled in categories as stated above, there will be no way to compare different school districts, schools, teachers, or children.

Evaluation of an educational program—whether at the national, state, local, or classroom level—is an attempt to determine what the instruction has accomplished. It cannot be completed, however, without goals or objectives as guideposts. Thus, a teacher must identify that which is to be the result of his instruction, plan the learning experience, expose the children to it, and then evaluate to determine the success of his program.

SELECTED REFERENCES

Berg, Harry, ed., *Evaluation in Social Studies*, 35th Yearbook. Washington, D.C.: National Council for the Social Studies, 1965.

Bloom, Benjamin S., ed., *Taxonomy of Educational Objectives: Cognitive Domain*. New York: David McKay Co., Inc., 1956.

Campbell, Vincent N. and Daryl G. Nichols, "National Assessment of Citizenship Education," *Social Education*, XXXII (March, 1968), 279.

Chase, W. Linwood, *A Guide for the Elementary Social Studies Teacher*. Boston: Allyn & Bacon, Inc., 1966.

Jarolimek, John and Huber M. Walsh, eds., *Readings for Social Studies in Elementary Education*. New York: The Macmillan Company, 1965.

Krathwohl, David R., Benjamin S. Bloom, and Bertram B. Mesia, *Taxonomy of Educational Objectives: Affective Domain*. New York: David McKay Co., Inc., 1964.

Kurfman, Dana, "A National Assessment of Social Studies Education," *Social Education*, XXXI (March, 1967), 209–11.

Michaelis, John U., ed., *Social Studies in Elementary Schools*. Washington, D.C.: National Council for the Social Studies, 1962.

Ragan, William B. and John D. McAulay, *Social Studies for Today's Children*. New York: Appleton-Century-Crofts, Inc., 1964.

[6]"A National Assessment of Social Studies Education," p. 209.

Index